# Piano
## on the Beach

*Pictures, Principles, and Perspectives for Success in Leadership and Life*

D0444310

# JIM DORNAN

© 2005  Network Twentyone

Additional copies of this book may be ordered from:
   Network Twentyone
   3550 Corporate Way, Suite C
   Duluth, GA  30096 USA

All rights reserved. No part of this publication may be reproduced, stored in a retrieval system, or transmitted in any form or by any means, electronic, mechanical, photocopies, recorded, or otherwise, except in the case of brief quotations embodied in critical articles or reviews, without the prior written permission of the publisher. First edition 2005.

Book Packaging and Design: W. B. Freeman Concepts, Tulsa, Oklahoma

Chapter Line-Art Illustrations: Royce Fitzgerald

Cover Design: Misenheimer.com

Printed in the United States of America
13 12 11 10 09 08 07 06 05    1 2 3 4 5

ISBN (paper): 0-9764913-0-3

# ABOUT
# THE AUTHOR

Jim Dornan is a leader of other leaders. As coach, strategist, and mentor for some of the highest achievers in the world, he has compiled a wealth of experiences, and a unique perspective that is available to any who choose to listen. As the father of three grown children, and with his wife, Nancy, as a life partner, Jim Dornan brings both business and personal views to his latest work.

A graduate of Purdue University who trained as an aeronautical engineer, Jim made the transition from the world of applied science to the world of entrepreneurial business more than thirty years ago. His enterprise, Network 21, is a global educational company that has been featured in *Success Magazine*, as well as the *Wall Street Journal*. He is the author of several best sellers, including *Becoming a Person of Influence*, which he co-wrote with John Maxwell. Jim speaks regularly to audiences of tens of thousands from Europe to Africa, India to Southeast Asia, and Australia to the Americas. He splits his time between residences in Florida and Georgia, but is at home in any of the twenty-five nations where he has offices and business friends.

# ACKNOWLEDGMENTS

As with any project that attempts to recall principles and experiences that might be helpful to others in their quest for a more significant and rewarding life, I have many people to thank:

- First and foremost, my wonderful wife of many years and life partner, Nancy. It was and is her remarkable passion and expectant spirit that kept me moving forward.

- My daughter, Heather, has been my partner in this project, and her input as well as her enthusiasm for my concepts have served as a necessary stimulant for the ultimate conquest of my procrastination on this work.

- My other children, David and Eric, have provided me endless experiences and stories upon which to test the theories of life and realities of leadership and influence.

- My granddaughter Ashley-Kate, for her remarkable ability to remind me of life's truths and priorities at the ripe age of four!

I am eternally grateful to so many people and leaders around the world that I have had the privilege of influencing, but who have influenced me in an even greater way. The things I have observed both in triumph and in despair have contributed mightily to a sense of wonder and excitement about the potential of every person in every circumstance. I remain humbled by the courage, the hunger to learn, and the endless creativity and resilience I see in everyday people. I am thankful to the Lord for giving me the privilege of participating as a fellow traveler and student.

# C O N T E N T S

# INTRODUCTION

# A Picture Is Worth a Thousand Words

They say a picture is worth a thousand words. In this book I want to plant some pictures in your mind—and then I'll even take a few thousand words to explain each one! Some of the most inspiring and helpful lessons I have learned in my life can be readily associated with a picture that embodies a principle. I'm excited to share these "life-lesson images" with you.

There are no magic formulas in this book. These are simple principles that work. The longer I'm in business, and perhaps the longer I live, the simpler success appears to me. Not easier...but *simpler.*

Upon entering engineering school in my early twenties, I had a number of theories and beliefs about success. They were all wrong. But who knew? There were no classes on leadership, entrepreneurship, or success offered by the college I attended. The basic curriculum covered English, history, math, science, and physical exercise. Later, I encountered courses in thermodynamics, calculus, rocket propulsion, statistics, and quantum physics. My colleagues studied such things as nursing, accounting, education, law, and medicine. These were great subjects, but there was nothing related to how to live a life of success and significance.

Through the years I have encountered four general theories that people seem to hold about success:

1. **Successful people are gifted or talented.** This is a common belief among people who don't have a focus for their life or any real understanding about the nature of their own gifts and talents. They see other people as being smarter or better, and they use this conclusion (based upon comparison) to justify their own lack of effort in developing and using the talents they DO have. The more I study successful people, the more I realize that talent, raw ability, and appearance have very little to do with success. Desire trumps talent every time.

**Desire trumps talent every time.**

2. **Successful people enjoy better circumstances.** So many people offer these excuses: no education or not enough education, no money or not enough money, no experience or not enough experience. They point to stiff competition, a health problem, a former bankruptcy, or an international war as excuses for why they can't succeed...and often for why they won't even TRY to succeed. Some say they are too young—try telling that to Bill Gates who started Microsoft at the age of nineteen. Some say they are too

old—try telling that to someone like Colonel Sanders who started Kentucky Fried Chicken after he was sixty-five years old. When dreams and desires are big enough, the facts related to circumstances don't count.

> **When dreams and desires are big enough, the facts related to circumstances don't count.**

3. **Successful people are lucky.** Some people assume that there are only so many "breaks" in the cosmos—and that they haven't had any. They believe that "if only" they had been at the right place, at the right time, talking to the right person, life would be different. Success is not a lottery and there is no limit to the number of successful people possible. Those who are truly successful will readily tell you that their luck began to turn the more they became mentally prepared to take on an opportunity. "Luck" showed up when they began to pursue a dream with all of their heart, mind, and soul, and to work diligently at achieving that dream. There is no whiffle dust that falls on some and not on others. Big dreams, noble goals, good attitudes, right values, and plain old-fashioned work are available to all!

4. **Successful people cheat.** There is actually a large number of people who believe that all successful people get rich by cheating, stealing, lying, or manipulating a system in some way. They simply do not believe that an honest, hard-working person can succeed. The facts don't support this thinking at all, of course. The vast majority of millionaires

are hard-working family people, or first-generation immigrant Americans, who own a small business, work hard every day, and save money to invest in business expansion. Greed and ambition may corrupt some people, but greedy and ambitious people nearly always crash their own ships on the rocks. They may be temporarily rich in money, but they rarely are wealthy in all areas of life that really matter.

If you truly want to be successful, you need to reject the four theories I have just stated. You need to seek out the REAL truths and principles that produce peace of mind and heart...security and freedom...love and honor...and a life of significance that adds value to other people.

My life adventure started in a small and unimpressive way. There was nothing spectacular about my early years. I eventually graduated from Purdue University and my wife, Nancy, and I moved to California to begin our careers. She was a speech therapist for a school district and I worked at designing commercial airliners at McDonnell Douglas (now Boeing). We were both working so many hours that we rarely saw each other—which was a major shock since we had seemed to be together constantly in college. My world felt oppressively negative and restrictive to me. When I looked at the lives of those above me on the corporate ladder...I did not at all want what they had. What a startling discovery it was to find that all of my training had directed me toward an industry in which I felt trapped!

So, we stepped out into the challenge of starting our own business. It was a small step at first, but I quickly discovered a whole new world. As an entrepreneur, I needed to build a marketing team and a client base. This was foreign territory to me. Nancy observed my behavior around people and quickly advised me to "rent a personality" if I wanted to proceed. She was right!

I started reading books to re-educate myself. The first two books I read had a profound impact on me—they were *The Magic of Thinking Big* by David Schwartz, and *How to Win Friends and Influence People* by Dale Carnegie.

I began to learn about what motivates people and the importance of attitude. I learned about goal setting, communication, and how to overcome fear. I felt as if I was discovering a secret treasure map. I read books by Maxwell Malz, Napoleon Hill, W. Clement Stone, and Norman Vincent Peale—then later, Zig Ziglar, John Maxwell, Dennis Waitley, Anthony Robbins, and literally hundreds of other authors. I attended seminars and listened to audio recordings.

I discovered that the world of business doesn't function on logic nearly as much as it functions on emotion. People want inspiration more than information. They want things to be simple. They want to be respected, listened to, and to have their accomplishments and good deeds recognized. There was so much I didn't know...and my education continues to this day. I still listen to CDs, read books, and have conversations almost daily with people who have done what I want to do or who can offer me some insight and perspective on how to take the next step I want to take.

> **I discovered that the world of business doesn't function on logic nearly as much as it functions on emotion.**

Through the years I have observed and assisted thousands of people who came from the worst circumstances, had the least obvious talent, were filled with the most fear, had experienced the worst luck, and who refused to cheat...and I have watched them succeed beyond their wildest dreams. I have also seen people who had great talent, fine circumstances, and everything going for them squander their potential or fail to overcome obstacles and complete a job. What a shame!

I have seen what a lack of integrity can do to someone with huge talent.

I have seen how much courage a simple, uneducated, but highly motivated person can display when faced with a huge problem.

I remain inspired and full of optimism about the potential in every person.

Our companies today produce millions of audio recordings in fifteen or more languages. We produce books, host websites globally, and conduct seminars around the world. All of these products and programs are grounded in a very SIMPLE message: Life is about loving, serving, empowering, and encouraging people.

**Life is about loving, serving, empowering, and encouraging people.**

We begin by loving, serving, empowering, and encouraging our own family members—and then we move out to our friends, neighbors, and close associates. Success is not so much a destination as it is a process. It is a way of thinking and living. And...it's available to you if you want it.

This book does not contain all the principles of success. But it contains the ones necessary for building a good foundation for success. If you are just starting out in pursuit of a new venture or dream, this book can be a primer for you. If you are well on your way to being a leader of others, you will find principles worthy of teaching and transferring to those you lead. If you are a parent, these are principles worthy of modeling and teaching to your children.

Principles, if true, should apply everywhere to people of all cultures, nations, and situations. We have found that the principles presented in this book meet that standard.

There's nothing complicated or overly difficult about:

- Dreaming big

- Praying for wisdom and humility

- Working hard

- Laughing more

- Keeping a positive attitude

- Believing in possibilities

or

- Pursuing a goal with all your heart, mind, and soul

If someone is going to be successful...why not you?

**What you see is what you get.**

**THE SCULPTURE**

A story is told about a large granite statue of a majestic horse rising up on its hind legs in anticipation of battle. People marveled at the skill required to produce this magnificent work of art, and were inspired by the commitment and passion of the sculptor. It was difficult to imagine how the beauty and raw power of this animal could have been created from what was originally a formless chunk of rock.

One day the sculptor was asked, "How were you able to produce such a refined work of art with only a small hammer and chisel?"

He replied, "Well, I just began as always with a large piece of rock. I visualized the object of my creation inside. Then I simply used the hammer and chisel to chip away at everything that did not belong in my mind's-eye version of the statue. Eventually, the horse was revealed as I had envisioned it."

Every time we begin a project or embark on a mission as a leader, we must first get a clear picture in our mind of the final outcome we desire. We need to be able to SEE what an excellent, successful, effective result *looks* like. Only then can we hope to navigate successfully through the distractions and obstacles we will encounter as we "chip away" at those things that do not fit our vision and goal.

This basic principle applies to personal as well as business goals. It applies to both short-term projects, and to major life or career decisions. We must ask:

- What do I ultimately want in order to feel that I have succeeded?

- What does the final goal LOOK like?

- What details will be in place in the final product?

- What will the ultimate description include?

Years ago I was told a story about a young man who was seeking advice from a trusted and wise teacher. He had expressed to his teacher a desire to have a life filled with purpose and fulfillment—a life that "truly mattered." The teacher asked, "What are your plans, young man?"

The young man replied, "I will complete my basic education and then go to the university."

The teacher asked, "And then what?"

The young man continued, "Then I will begin my career and get married."

The teacher again asked, "And then what?"

The young man said with enthusiasm, "Then I will work hard and improve my financial situation and start a family."

The teacher said, "And then what?"

The young man was beginning to get a little frustrated at the continual repetition of his teacher's question. He said, "I guess I will build wealth and raise my children and think about retirement."

The teacher continued to probe, "And then what?"

The young man said with growing exasperation, "Well, I guess then I will get old and die."

The teacher asked with a sigh, "And then what?"

The young man was thoroughly puzzled and after a few moments of deep thought said quietly, "I don't know after that."

The teacher replied, "Young man, until you have answered that one final question, the others are not very important."

Is this lifetime the sum of a person's existence? Is this all there is? If so, perhaps pleasure and material success are the only games in town. If beauty and money and power are the ultimate goals, then the means of achieving these pursuits are rather clear, and unfulfilling. But...if there is something after life...if there is a deeper purpose...if there is value beyond the temporary earning of money and promotions on a corporate ladder...then our first and foremost challenge is to answer the "and after death, then what?" question.

Many definitions of success focus on the four Ps: Pleasure, Power, Prosperity, and Popularity. Advertisers and media programs celebrate the "beautiful people" and depict the powerful and wealthy as "having it all." Yet again and again we see evidence that these are the very people who seem to be plagued by troubles and unrest. Lawsuits, suicides, drugs, and divorce are considered "normal" in the lives of those people our modern society often holds up as successful.

Does this mean that success is bad? Does it mean money and power are wrong? Does it indicate that the price of success is too high?

No. I strongly believe it is possible to have real purpose and allow money to be a tool for fulfilling that purpose. In the hands of someone with strong values and noble purpose, wealth and influence can be powerful forces for good. What is required is a new definition of success according to higher values! We need to set our priorities with the end game in mind. We need to make our daily choices and our intermediate goals line up with the "final result" that we envision in our minds.

> **In the hands of someone with strong values and noble purpose, wealth and influence can be powerful forces for good.**

In the end, success isn't nearly as important as significance. Begin to think in terms of significance. What really COUNTS? What really MATTERS? What will be the hallmarks of your life that become your LEGACY and your ultimate REPUTATION?

Nearly every person I know would consider this to be a good starting profile for a life of significance:

- Strong faith

- A good and solid marriage

- Good health

- Strong family relationships

- Material success based on hard work and right thinking

- A deep sense of satisfaction that your time and effort have been spent in the pursuit of noble values and high ideals

The person who lives a life with these characteristics may not be at the top of the organizational chart...or that person may be! The person who lives a life with this profile may not be a multimillionaire...or that person may be! The person may not be recognized as a social leader...or that person may be! One thing is certain: A person who lives with this profile of SIGNIFICANCE will be a person who is a sure winner in his or her own heart and mind, and in the hearts and minds of beloved family members and friends.

Without a clear picture of where you want to be and who you want to be, your life will become reactionary at best, and at worst, be driven by shallow pursuits that eventually leave you feeling empty, dissatisfied, and unfulfilled. ·

## Life Is a Sum of Choices

Life is filled with choices. Some choices are small ones. Others are bigger, such as: "Who will I marry?"; "Will I have children?"; "What will be my career or profession?"; and "What are my spiritual beliefs and core values?" As one person put it, "We only know the difference between small choices and bigger ones in hindsight." A choice to turn left instead of right can mean a great deal when the intersection is a major one, such as whether a person will go to college or take a particular job.

Some choices are subject to change over time. Others should be choices that are non-negotiable regardless of circumstances. These latter choices should definitely include a person's choices about spiritual beliefs and core values.

Some choices are "reactionary" to circumstances—in other words, we make a choice after something has happened that was beyond our control. Other choices are ones that CREATE circumstances.

One of the most important choices I believe a person can make is the choice of a spouse. I believe that to be successful, a person must make a decision, and then work from a position of total commitment to "adding value" to the other partner. As we seek to serve and to love someone else, we see real love grow deeper and become more satisfying. Too many people divorce simply because they have a concept of love that is based on feelings and circumstances, rather than on "committed choice."

Years ago I read an article about a very high-profile movie star, an action hero, who divorced his wife after the birth of their child. The child suffered from autism and had severe problems. When this man was asked about the reason for his divorce, he said, "After our child and all the problems...it was no longer fun."

What a terrible reason for a divorce! Actually, I have no real idea what was happening in their life and marriage, but the comment was one typical of what we hear every day: "I just don't *feel* the same" or, "I found someone else that treats me better" or, "I have more fun with someone else."

> **A life rooted in clear values, purpose, and commitment is solid and steadfast.**

A life in which choices are driven by circumstances and emotions is easily blown about from relationship to relationship, career to career, and usually, from failure to failure.

A life rooted in clear values, purpose, and commitment is solid and steadfast. It produces *significance* that embodies success in all dimensions of life: spiritual life, relational and emotional life, and material and financial life.

When our son Eric was born, our life became quite complicated for a number of years. Eric was born with spina bifida, which is a birth defect in which the spinal cord does not form correctly. Many complications usually accompany the birth of a spina bifida baby. Eric's situation was complicated in that the physician did not notice the condition at delivery and therefore the open spine and the spinal fluid were contaminated. This led to meningitis, which led to surgery after surgery. Eric had eleven brain surgeries that first year of his life. A shunt was put in place to drain fluid from his brain directly into his abdominal area, and this tubing remains necessary even today. We were not able to bring him home from the hospital for nine months after his birth. That was quite a year!

Our daughter, Heather, was four-and-a-half years old at the time Eric was born. Our financial life was very unstable in our new business. Our lives seemed to be pulled in a dozen directions and we felt extremely vulnerable to every kind of disaster. We needed to balance our days between the care of Heather at home and Eric in the hospital. We needed to balance work time and hospital time. We needed more money than ever before and had less time to earn it. We faced enormous hospital bills since our little insurance policy didn't cover anything after the first week of Eric's hospitalization. The strain on our marriage was immense. Statistics say that the birth of a handicapped baby results in the divorce of the baby's parents more than eighty-five percent of the time. We were committed NOT to be part of that statistic!

**Part of the clear vision that we set for our life was to provide a loving and stable home for our children and to have a loving and committed marriage.**

Nancy and I faced other choices. We determined NOT to give up...on ANY aspect of our life together! We determined to work through our pain, and to work through the strain, and to work through the issues of blame, and to emerge stronger than ever. Part of the clear vision that we set for our life was to *provide a loving and stable home for our children* and to have a *loving and committed marriage.*

Was it easy? No.

Was it worth it? YES!

Was it a choice we made—a choice rooted in values and commitment? Absolutely.

We not only needed to make choices related to our marriage and family, we needed to make choices related to our finances. Nancy and I both wanted a good quality of life for our family. We certainly did not want a life that was ruled by staggering indebtedness to a hospital and physicians. We did not want a life marked by bankruptcy or poverty. We knew that we needed to make some serious choices about HOW we were going to afford the best health care possible and provide a quality lifestyle for our children. We also faced choices about how to manage our time.

We CHOSE to focus on solutions, not obstacles.

We CHOSE to envision a future in which we had everything we valued, and in proper balance.

We CHOSE to take what had been given to us as a circumstance and turn it into the success we envisioned.

Our vision for a life of abundance and purpose was eventually fulfilled. It didn't happen overnight, but it did happen. Nancy and I have been married more than thirty-seven years at the writing of this book. Our children are grown. We have a career that gives us genuine wealth—not only in terms of money but in terms of purpose, fulfillment, and satisfaction.

Certainly I am not diminishing the value of money. Money doesn't buy happiness...but neither does poverty. I have been very poor and I have been wealthy, and I prefer wealthy. As a person with adequate resources I have more options, and less of my time needs to be spent in supplying life's essentials or in dealing with the frustrations that arise when options are limited. I am thankful for the memories we have been able to create and for the things we have been able to provide for our family and others. Money is a wonderful tool for accomplishing things rooted in lasting purpose. Just as success is not the same as significance, so money is not the same as wealth.

Nancy and I chose to pursue a life that was significant and wealthy in all the things that truly MATTER to us: our faith in God, our family, our friends, and our commitment to helping others in need.

> **Just as success is not the same as significance, so money is not the same as wealth.**

If I had to sum up the three key principles that have been the heart of our "committed choices" through the years they would be these:

- Faith in a God who loves us
- Focus on a positive, productive life
- Refusal to be distracted by circumstances

I have absolutely no doubt that these principles can and will work for anyone who knows what they desire to achieve by the end of their life, and who is willing to make the right choices daily to pursue their value-based goals.

## What Do YOU Envision as Fulfilling and Rewarding?

Take a few moments to reflect upon what you truly find fulfilling and rewarding. What do you believe a "fulfilled" and "well-rewarded" life might look like ten, twenty, thirty or more years down the line? How do you define a life of SIGNIFICANCE...and not just success?

Someone once said that we don't get from life what we deserve, but we usually get what we expect. The Bible says this same thing: From everyone to whom much is given, much will be required.[1]

---

**We don't get from life what we deserve, but we usually get what we expect.**

---

Does this scare you? It shouldn't. I hope you will think big and expect a great life of happiness and abundance. I believe it is wonderful and noble to believe for a TREMENDOUSLY significant and wealthy life in all ways that are truly meaningful and purposeful.

Begin to get a vivid picture in your mind about what you want life to look like two to five years from now, and then ten years from now. Don't just see yourself as comfortable and free of pain. See yourself accomplishing things that truly matter. Recognize that a significant life will be one that includes some memories of "challenges met" and "obstacles overcome"—a truly significant life may have problems, but it should not have any regrets.

Let your choices and your picture of your own future guide your daily decisions.

As circumstances arise and distractions come your way, chip away at anything that doesn't fit your ultimate vision for your own significance and worth.

## Forming a Picture in Your Mind

But how, you may be asking, can I get this picture in my mind?

If you don't have a clear picture of what you want your future to be like, you perhaps need to go back to the picture you had at some earlier point in your life about what your future would be like. Did you imagine living in a certain home...surrounded by family and friends...having achieved a particular goal...working in a particular career...having a sense of purpose and value?

That early dream is likely to be your current dream—it just may have faded a bit! You may need to dust off that dream and begin to hold it out before you again as a strong, clear, and persistent vision for your future.

Perhaps you have never had a clear mental vision about your own significance. Today is the day to develop one.

Keep in mind, too, that a picture of your future can develop and come into greater focus as time passes.

**A truly significant life may have problems, but it should not have any regrets.**

About fifteen years ago I spoke to nearly twenty-five thousand people at a convention of men and women who were developing their own businesses. I spoke to them on leadership and success principles. After that conference, I had a strong desire to someday assemble a group like that of my own associates and teammates.

Up to that point, I had never been able to gather together more than about two thousand of my own associates. There's a major difference in the budget and planning for an event involving two thousand people and one involving twenty-five thousand people! Even so, I dreamed of having such an event to showcase the very best and brightest people in my own business. I dreamed of an audience of more than twenty thousand people. I could SEE such an event in my mind's eye...it was a great event as I visualized it! My mental picture was strong, vividly detailed, and crystal-clear.

About that same time, I had decided after urgent "encouragement" from my wife, Nancy, to expand our business educational activities into the international arena. Our first ventures on the international stage had been small and were marked by a few difficulties, but we had managed to set up offices in a few markets and our numbers were growing. I began to SEE a growing international market and to pursue it.

To make a very long story short, we eventually found ourselves with offices in more than twenty nations in Europe, Africa, Asia, and Australia. We began conducting seminars and producing resource materials in the local languages in each of these regions of the world. The numbers of hungry, teachable, and thankful people grew and grew. Their stories were and are deeply inspiring.

And...we experienced an attendance of fifty thousand people at my first event in Hungary! Then we saw twenty thousand in attendance at an event in Poland. We had similar numbers in other places throughout Eastern Europe.

Eventually we saw twenty thousand people attend our event at an outdoor soccer stadium in Indonesia. About forty thousand came to a similar event in Mumbai (Bombay), India, and on and on it has gone.

One event in Indonesia was especially memorable. Nancy and I watched in amazement as seven thousand people remained in their seats for two days of meetings in an OUTDOOR stadium during a major tropical rainstorm! That's commitment.

Hundreds of thousands of people on our team are now engaged worldwide in learning and growing, both in business and in life. My vision has become a reality!

We have world-class speakers and entertainers. We have high-quality educational material and we create extremely inspirational environments. Let me assure you, as I look out on the audiences to which I speak today, they look amazingly like the twenty-five thousand people I saw before me fifteen years ago!

The reality is actually much greater than my original vision. We are reaching more than 250,000 people every few months, not just 25,000.

We are global, not limited to one nation. We are in more than fifteen languages—from Hindi to Mandarin to Turkish to Russian.

What I saw in my MIND's eye is now what I see with my NATURAL eyes. What happened in my life can happen in yours.

# The Life You WANT to Lead

This principle of SEEING your goals being met works in all areas of life.

For many years, my wife, Nancy, and I dreamed about having a second home on the beach. This was a particular passion of Nancy's. The vision for a second home represented peace, freedom, and a place to reflect on life.

A number of years ago we leased a home in Hawaii near Diamond Head, just a few miles from Waikiki Beach. The home was fine and our children had a great month there with us. Down the beach, however, was a MAGNIFICENT home. It was unique in that it had a large amount of green grass beautifully manicured and extending all the way from the house to the sand. The yard of that home looked like a park. Nancy moved to a new level in her vision for a beach home!

> **This principle of SEEING your goals being met works in all areas of life.**

Nancy has always loved big expansive decks where a person or groups of people might sit in the shade under a fan and watch the ocean. She added to her vision of a deck the idea of seeing park-like grass beyond the deck, and beyond the grass, sand and ocean. Our motto became: "Deck, grass, sand, water."

Over the next several years we traveled to a number of exotic locations, including Hawaii, the Caribbean, the Great Barrier Reef, and places in Greece, Italy, and France overlooking the Mediterranean Sea. We looked at beach real estate in Hawaii, Florida, and California. Every time Nancy saw a nice place, she would say, "Where is the deck-grass-sand-water?" Some of the places had a deck and sand...some had water and grass...some had water and a deck...some had grass but no sand. None of these were just as she had pictured it. She had visualized it ALL, not just part. So we kept looking.

Then came the day a few years ago when we were looking for a place to lease for a year as we set up our residency in the state of Florida. We were taken to a home that caught us by surprise. We entered the gate to a large piece of property right on the ocean and went inside. As we walked out onto the large deck at the rear of the house, we saw something amazing: a one-acre, beautifully mowed lawn extending from the house right down to the sand and the water. Deck, grass, sand, water—Nancy had found her beach home!

I had no choice from that moment on. We HAD to buy the house. If the owner or realtor had known how much we wanted the house, I'm sure they would have been able to get more money for it. We just HAD to have it—it fit the picture perfectly. The somewhat-humorous part of this story is that after we took ownership, we completely remodeled the interior of the house, moving walls and significantly changing the kitchen and the bathrooms. Actually, the only "original" part of the house remaining after the remodeling was the deck—to the grass, sand, and water. The aspects of the house that were irreplaceable were not changed. Everything else was open to negotiation and change.

So it must be in life's choices when it comes to pursuing real significance and genuine wealth. There are some choices and some aspects of life that are irreplaceable. Those are the areas that must not be changed. Other areas that are not of lasting, significant value can be "chipped away"—in some cases, those areas *need* to be chipped away.

What is your dream life?

Can you see it vividly?

What will give your life significance? What will give you a feeling that you have accomplished ALL that you were put on this earth to accomplish? What will give you a feeling of being truly "wealthy"—regardless of how much money you may amass?

## Do You Have a "Life Sentence"?

When your dream life is fully and vividly envisioned, you should be able to sum it up in one sentence. Stop to think for a moment. Someday as people are discussing your life at a family gathering or in a meeting of people in your organization, what will they say? What was your purpose? What was your passion? What will they say about you?

My granddaughter Ashley-Kate loves to work jigsaw puzzles. She is only four years old so she isn't working the thousand-piece puzzles yet. She only works the basic ones for young children. We always begin to work the puzzle by setting the box cover in front of us. I love to watch her try to find the right pieces and put them together. There's one particular puzzle that shows a bunny on a bicycle. It has only about twenty pieces.

Ashley-Kate usually starts with the pieces that relate to the bunny since he is the most obvious figure in the puzzle. The blue sky and flowers are harder. Each time she takes a piece in her hand, she looks at the box cover to see how the colors fit together. One thing I've noticed is that each time we work that puzzle, Ashley-Kate completes it in a little less time.

Can you imagine trying to put together a very difficult and intricate jigsaw puzzle without a picture? The more complex the puzzle, the more important it is to have a picture for reference.

Putting together the odd-shaped pieces of various experiences so everything fits...carving out a life from nothing...is a far greater challenge than any puzzle! A clear vision is absolutely critical to achieving significance.

> **A clear vision is absolutely critical to achieving significance.**

The sooner you have a picture of what you want to be and do in your life, and the clearer that picture is, the simpler your life will become. Decisions will be easier, distractions will be less distracting, and your passion will be more focused. When you decide with a firm commitment who you will live with...and what you want to accomplish in your business or career...and what spiritual beliefs and values will be at the core of your life...you will find that most of life's daily decisions are easy to make. They will simply fit into place. You will know what to hold on to, and what to chip away or let go.

Let me recommend to you today:

- Decide the big things.

- Form a clear picture of what you want and where you are going.

- Don't let other things or people distract you.

- Chip away and reject what does not fit your picture.

- Keep looking at the "box cover" of your vision for your life to see if you are on track.

**The most important things are beneath the surface.**

**T H E   I C E B E R G**

T he first time I saw an iceberg up close was during a week-long cruise aboard a beautiful private yacht in the coastal waterways near Juneau, Alaska. Our yacht was an impressive one hundred and ten feet in length and we felt as if we were the "king of the sea." Then we sailed up to the Mendenhall Glacier and passed by several amazing icebergs. We could *feel* the power of their presence.

The wall of this glacier is immense, but even the smaller pieces of flakier ice floating near us were many times the size of our yacht. We knew, however, that the real power, and danger, was in the part we could not see—it was below the surface.

Everyone has heard the tragic story of the Titanic. Although there has been much controversy and discussion through the years about how this reportedly unsinkable ship could have met such a sad fate, what we do know with certainty is that one thousand, five hundred

PIANO ON THE BEACH

...three souls were lost on that fateful night of April 14, 1912. Reports indicate that at least five separate warnings were given on that crystal-clear night just before the huge ship struck the iceberg with its forty-six thousand tons of steel. It took only thirty minutes for that state-of-the-art ship to sink into the icy-cold waters of the north Atlantic.

Having seen an iceberg up close, let me assure you that an iceberg is a beautiful sight to behold as the ice glistens in the sun. What isn't seen—the ninety percent of the iceberg that is underneath the water—is what can be deadly.

## People Are Like Icebergs

In many ways people are like icebergs. The appearance of a person—including the skills and talents that are evident in work produced or performances given—is only about ten percent of who the person really is. Character—the far greater and more important part of a person—lies below the surface. And it is that part that can sink a life.

> **Character— the far greater and more important part of a person—lies below the surface. And it is that part that can sink a life.**

We must always have a healthy respect for the things that lie below the surface of life. We need to spend more of our time working on the ninety percent of our being that isn't readily seen by others...and less time on those surface attributes that are far less important in the long run. The "sizzle" on the surface is never nearly as important as the "substance" underneath.

I encourage you to reflect for a few moments on some of the recent scandals in corporate America—for example, incidents involving Enron, Tyco, and MCI/WorldCom. Executives, entrusted to be stewards of the shareholders' and employees' assets, behaved disgracefully. These executives had talent, skill, and drive to reach the top, but they allowed their greed, egos, and a distorted sense of values to lead them into dishonorable behavior. Their actions resulted in billions of lost dollars and countless thousands of people losing their jobs. A few leaders with weak character took down large corporations and sent their "dependents" into the cold and murky waters of bankruptcy, ruined careers, and lost retirement funds.

> **The "sizzle" on the surface is never nearly as important as the "substance" underneath.**

In the case of Enron, the public accounting firm of Arthur Andersen allowed irregularities to go unreported and even validated irregularities with what has come to be called "creative accounting." Contributing to the character flaws of another person is also a character flaw!

Short-term success was elevated. Character and values were kept below the surface. And in the end, giant corporate "ships" were sunk.

Let's consider for a few moments the case of Dennis Kozlowski of Tyco, a chief executive officer well-known in the corporate world for living a lavish, irresponsible, and reckless personal life. The suit filed against Kozlowski by the United States Securities and Exchange Commission (SEC) cited improper loans totaling more than $315 million. The SEC charged that Kozlowski used this loan money to amass millions of dollars' worth of fine art, yachts, and estate jewelry, as well as property in New York City and a palatial estate on Nantucket Island.

Other improperly secured corporate funds allegedly were used by Kozlowski for lavish events, such as the party he threw for his wife on the island of Sardinia. Investigators obtained an e-mail from party planner Beth Pacitti that read, "We'll have a lion or a horse with a chariot, for the shock value, and two gladiators to meet guests at the door."

According to authorities, Kozlowski allegedly pillaged a fund Tyco used to help executives relocate in order to buy his first wife, Angie, a $7 million Park Avenue apartment. One top executive dipped into the fund to buy a $6.5 million Upper East Side Manhattan apartment, and another used $14 million to buy a Central Park West unit and a ski chalet in Utah.

Kozlowski allegedly billed Tyco $72,042 for jewelry, $155,067 for clothing, $96,943 for flowers, $60,427 for club memberships, $52,334 for wine, and $110,000 for corporate use of his personal yacht.

What is especially sad to me is that Kozlowski and other executives like him are people with great talent, ambition, and discipline. They have reached the pinnacle of corporate life—not on a whim but as the result of hard work, driving zeal, and clear goals. They are people who developed their business ability to its maximum level. What they FAILED to do was to develop their character and integrity. They eventually placed their own egos and desire for comfort and luxury ahead of their responsibilities as leaders.

> **People of character don't take advantage of position and power.**

People of character don't take advantage of position and power.

People of character don't put their careers ahead of stewardship of company or public money.

People of character don't violate their own basic core values in order to have parties with lions and horses and gladiators at the door.

# The Danger of a Character Deficiency

A hundred years ago a young boy named Schicklewuber grew up in Europe without being taught right from wrong. He was insulted and put down every time he voiced his ambitions of becoming a priest, or perhaps an artist. No one taught him or modeled good values, and therefore, he didn't acquire good values. This boy was convinced that his parents did not love him so he ran away, emotionally scarred and with a very poor character foundation. Amazingly—especially considering the environment from which he came—he rose to become a man of great power and influence. He changed his name, and history knows him as Adolf Hitler.

Hitler had lots of talents and many skills, especially communication skills. He was highly ambitious. He had a natural charisma that was attractive on the outside. His giant character flaws are what led to the eventual murder of millions of people.

As I have read history I have been struck by the fact that nearly all evil and destructive people who had a major influence on the world were people who had tremendous talent and the ability to attract and influence others. They had skills related to their goals and at times they even engaged in heroic actions. Then, suddenly, their character was exposed to reveal a self-serving agenda and rotten values. Their deep character flaws caused them to "implode" and to engage in highly destructive behavior.

Talent plus charisma plus accomplishment *without character* is a dangerous combination...not only to the individual marked by these traits but to countless others.

# How Firm Is Your Foundation?

Have you ever witnessed the building of a skyscraper? When I visit large cities such as New York City, or the great and growing Asian cities of Kuala Lumpur, Malaysia, or Shanghai, China, I marvel at the construction of these giant structures. I've noticed that it often takes months, even years, to lay the foundation for a tall building. Why? Because the higher the building is designed to become, the deeper the foundation must be laid. Extensive calculations are done to determine the forces that an earthquake or storm might have on a skyscraper, and rollers are installed far below the surface so the building can absorb those forces and avoid substantial damage or collapse.

> **Talent plus charisma plus accomplishment *without character* is a dangerous combination.**

After the foundation is set, it may only take a few months to construct the entire "above-ground" part of the building. The skyscraper we see is never the FULL building. The real power and strength of the building lie below the surface.

The same is true for good leaders and long-term achievers.

We all know the story of the Three Little Pigs. One built a house with straw, one with sticks, and one with bricks. The house built with bricks took longer to construct, but when the Big Bad Wolf came along huffing and puffing, only the brick house remained standing. We need to take the time to build brick houses in our character.

The Bible tells us to build our houses on rock rather than sand.[2]

Storms and earthquakes are inevitable in life. Big bad wolves are still huffing and puffing. We can only survive and thrive if we build our lives on a strong and solid foundation of good character.

Some people think that the foundation of a good character is laid in early childhood and is never adjusted or further developed after a person becomes an adult. That simply is not so. A foundation in early childhood can be eroded...or it can be strengthened. We as adults must take responsibility for our own character development and continue to strengthen our character all the days of our lives! Nobody will *force* you as an adult to develop an outstanding character or to be a person of great integrity and high moral values. YOU must be the prime architect of your own character refinement.

**YOU must be the prime architect of your own character refinement.**

In all of my years of study at Purdue University, I do not remember a class that dealt with character issues. We were taught complex math formulas and aerodynamic design principles...but not how to be a person of character. It was as though character didn't matter, or perhaps the assumption was made that a person automatically had either a good character or a bad one. Character was never even mentioned on the list of "ingredients for success."

Thousands of books line our library and bookstore shelves, telling us how to sell, negotiate, manage, and communicate. Degrees and diplomas are readily available in computer science, accounting, medicine, law, and finance. There are courses and classes about how to dress for success, speak publicly, design résumés, conduct a skillful interview, set goals, and engage in long-range and short-range planning. However, without character undergirding these important skills and abilities, we can end up with a surface success that breaks down at the first sign of pressure or stress.

To truly develop and maintain character, a person must form personal values and habits based on timeless truths and a respect for others. The process is lifelong, and it must be intentional. Good character doesn't happen by accident. Integrity doesn't happen automatically over time. You must make a deliberate choice to become a person of integrity and to strengthen your character values.

Where do we begin in bolstering our own character? I believe the secret lies in this saying:

Sow a thought...reap an act.

Sow an act...reap a habit.

Sow a habit...reap a character.

Sow a character...reap a destiny.

**Skills, personality, driving motivation, and talent may get you to the top, but it is character that will keep you there.**

Character begins with what you think. Character is rooted in daily habits, including habits in thinking. Character is a summation of how we think and act day in and day out, over years and decades. Character is another word for long-term thinking and long-term habits!

Skills, personality, driving motivation, and talent may get you to the top, but it is character that will keep you there.

## Long-Term Thinking

Never be fooled by the apparent success of someone who seems to reach the top quickly or who has gained their fifteen minutes of national fame. Quick success often is followed by a quick downfall. A house of cards can be put up quickly, but it collapses with the first strong gust of wind. Profound achievement, lasting fame, and strong leadership are built over time.

I like this expression my wife, Nancy, uses often: "The longest distance between two points is the shortcut." When we ignore time-honored rules and adjust our behavior to create instant success, we nearly always end up with disastrous results. What leads a person to seek a shortcut? There are three main reasons that come to mind:

> **"The longest distance between two points is the shortcut."**

1. **Ego.** A person may have an out-of-control competitive spirit or desire to achieve "at all costs."

2. **Pride.** A person may have a great fear of embarrassment or failure. This can lead a person to "fudge" results or adjust the truth to remain on top.

3. **A False Definition of Success.** A person may believe that appearance is everything. Such a person often will manipulate a situation and adopt a winner-take-all attitude in all things so that the end ALWAYS seems to justify the means—and the end, in this person's case, is the appearance of winning. A person who has a false definition of success usually believes that he who has the most toys, wins.

The truth is that people with super-sized egos...people who are proud...and people who routinely manipulate others to ensure their own victories...nearly always lose in the long run! Deceitful behavior and self-serving shortcuts never pay off in terms of solid significance.

Take a look at those who have tried these shortcuts and you will conclude that in the long run of their lives, their moral failures, financial dishonesty, exaggerated results, and unreported errors eventually caught up with them and that their "end" was destructive and disastrous. Only those who are honest and stick to high-character principles survive with integrity and have a reputation that inspires future generations.

# Conduct Your Own Character Assessment

How can you tell if you need some bolstering in character? Conduct a personal review of your habits and actions. Ask yourself the questions below. Have you ever:

- Exaggerated the features or benefits of your product or service to close on a sale?

- Misled a client in discrediting your competition to give yourself an edge?

- Misrepresented facts on your résumé to hide a major failure?

- Taken credit for reaching a goal (such as a sales target, budget, growth percentage, or new client acquisition) when the actual results were still in question, or when you were NOT the sole person or even the leader charged with achieving the goal?

- Manipulated dollar figures or statistics to your advantage?

- Enhanced, exaggerated, or distorted your achievements to appear more interesting or successful to others?

- Misrepresented income or expenses at tax time, or on an expense report?

- Failed to claim something on a customs form after an international trip?

- Gone somewhere and then lied about it?

- Repeated something told to you in confidence?
- Accepted money or a prize you didn't really earn?

Do these questions sound harsh or unrealistic? The truth is, character is what and who you are when no one is looking!

Character is the foundation for self-esteem. Even if you "get away with it," YOU know what you have done. Character is what makes you trustworthy in your own eyes, and being trustworthy is a critical factor in leadership. Trust is far more of a factor in leadership than position, personality, or the power of influence. Indeed, trust is the first key element of leadership and influence.

**Character is the foundation for self-esteem.**

If you know deep within that you are not trustworthy, over time you will project your own lack of trustworthiness to others. No matter how hard you try to hide the real truth of your character, it eventually will be revealed!

Like an iceberg, the ninety percent of you that is character is what will hold up your skills, talents, and other aspects of outward appearance—the ten percent that is "show." It is your character that ultimately allows you to shine in ways that are lasting—in good times and bad.

**Discover the gold inside.**

**THE GOLDEN BUDDHA**

For many years an eight-foot-tall concrete Buddha sat conspicuously in the middle of Bangkok, Thailand. It was not, however, an admired object of art, nor did people give it any respect as a religious object. Visitors from around the world often placed their empty soda cans on it, used it to hold their cameras while they changed film, or generally ignored it.

Then one day about forty years ago a Buddhist priest took the old statue to his temple. During the moving process, the statue cracked. As various pieces fell off, the priest noticed something shining beneath the concrete. With the help of others, he pulled away all of the concrete shell and discovered the world's largest chunk of sculptured gold.

The statue was of immense value! And the value was there all the time.

What a classic case of significance missed...beauty obscured... potential unrealized! What an example of an underutilized asset!

Each one of us knows people who have gold inside of them, but it's currently hiding under a concrete covering. You may even know that about yourself.

# The Tremendous Value of YOU

Every person has unique, God-given talents and potential. One of the most difficult things to achieve and maintain in life, however, is a healthy and positive respect for what we have and who we are. Millions of people live with a poor self-image because they do not place value on what lies inside themselves. They see only their exterior failures, not their internal worth. They have allowed their genuine gifts and abilities to be coated over with a hardened shell of doubt and insecurity. They are quick to pursue the latest fad in order to *appear* confident and worthy.

A truly healthy self-image is not about pleasing others or following popular trends. It is about knowing who you are, what you are made of on the inside, where you are going, and what you stand for. It's about discovering your strengths and gifts, and learning how to accept or control your weaknesses.

A healthy self-image is not about perfection—it is about being the best you can be.

A healthy self-image is not about winning a competition or engaging in comparisons with others—it is about doing all you can do.

When a person truly has a healthy self-image, that person has:

- A sense of balance
- A sense of purpose

- A sense of humor about successes and failures
- A strength that is much deeper and less fragile than the latest fad

# Which Psychological Position Do You Take?

In working with people from various cultures over the years, I have observed three key psychological positions that influence daily behavior:

1. **Superiority.** Those who see themselves as superior do not admit to any weakness or flaw. They project themselves as being the strongest, smartest, most cool, and most successful person in a group.

   This position may be positive, but it is not healthy.

2. **Inferiority.** Those who see themselves as inferior see the strengths of others but not their own strengths. They conclude that they are less talented, less attractive, and less successful than others to whom they compare themselves. They desire the qualities they see in others and know they lack, but they have little genuine hope of attaining those qualities. They see their natural gifts and abilities as being insignificant.

   This position is neither positive nor healthy.

3. **Balanced.** Those who see themselves as balanced know that they have God-given strengths and gifts that can be used to pursue their goals. They acknowledge the gifts of others without fear of reducing their own value. They work

on improving themselves, but have no illusions about perfection.

This position is healthy and positive, and it will lead to a life of significance and satisfaction.

## Our Great Need to "Measure Up"

Each of us has a certain degree of pride. We have an ego. We want to be seen by others as being strong, attractive, and successful. We also, however, seem to have a built-in tendency to focus more on our weaknesses than on our strengths, and to minimize our gifts.

**Balanced people acknowledge the gifts of others without fear of reducing their own value.**

Some people seem to be continually and painfully aware of their weaknesses and failures. They rehearse them over and over in their minds. They are overly conscious of, and perhaps overly awed by, the strengths they see in others they admire. They put others on a pedestal and contrast their own failings with the success of others. In that type of scenario, a person hardly ever measures up.

Those who are bound up by their "inside negatives" need to realize that these negative views of their own abilities didn't just come into their minds and hearts out of thin air. They weren't born feeling this way about themselves. Some people believe the environment in which they lived as a child is at fault...the comments of their parents are at fault...that some people simply have more good qualities than other people...and even that the position of the moon or stars had something to do with their perceptions. In truth, however, the negative opinions a person has of his or her own abilities are *primarily* a product of his or her own experiences—both successes and failures—and his or her own "self-talk" about those experiences.

Our first feelings of inadequacy tend to strike us when we are very young, usually from a childhood embarrassment that might still haunt us. Most of us could make a list without thinking twice. We recall taunts from schoolmates, parents, or teachers. Were you called "chubby" or "skinny"? (A person can't win when it comes to weight!) Were you "four-eyes," a "loser," or a "geek"? Did someone make fun of your hair, your eyes, your skin, your ears, your quietness, your laugh, your teeth, your legs, or your nose? (Isn't it all pretty silly now?) When a person carries the baggage of those criticisms over time, that baggage becomes part of the person's overall self-image. It's both common and unfortunate.

We tend to remember every rejection, every embarrassment, and every nickname as though we were dragging it along behind us on a string. The irony is that oftentimes, the person who said or did something that tacked a "label" on us very typically doesn't remember ever doing so!

## Who Are We Trying to Please?

In the end, we need to ask a very simple question: "Who am I trying to please?"

Most people spend far too much time thinking about what others think. In truth, others think about you far less than you can imagine! Have you ever noticed how a person will look at a group picture and say only, "That's a horrible picture of me"? Nothing is said about anybody else in the group! We often have an obsession with our own image. We spend hours in any given year just thinking, *My hair isn't right* or, *I look fat*. We rarely, however, look at other people in a group picture, and say, "She looks fat" or, "Her hair isn't right." We EACH tend to focus on our own appearance and have little concern for the appearance of others—and at the same time, think the whole world is judging how we look! We can be strangely self-critical, and it doesn't have to be logical at all.

> **If we are pursuing perfection as the definition of success, then we will be comparing ourselves constantly with an unreachable ideal.**

Our obsession with self is related to our definition of success. If we are pursuing perfection as the definition of success, then we will be comparing ourselves constantly with an unreachable ideal. We will have an ever-present concern with whether we are "perfect"—or not.

If we are pursuing "winning" as our definition of success, then we will be comparing ourselves constantly to others in a competitive way. We will have an ever-present concern with how WE are doing compared to a close rival or competitor.

In the end, nobody is perfect and nobody wins all the time. An obsession with self alone results in deep feelings of discouragement and frustration!

Rather than focus on others or on perfection, we need to focus on developing inner qualities that truly will attract others and win their respect. To lay a foundation for long-term success and happiness, we need to be concerned more with who we ARE using internal, character-based criteria, and less concerned with how we APPEAR to others based on external criteria. We need to take responsibility for defining ourselves according to what we truly believe is important, and for evaluating and developing our strengths so they become dominant over any weaknesses we may have.

Self-image may be influenced by what others have said or didn't say—or by what others have done or failed to do. We need to recognize that others, however, do not have the FINAL say. We are the ones who can have the final say about our own value and worth. We are the ones who determine the final outcome based upon what we choose to do.

**In the end, nobody is perfect and nobody wins all the time.**

# Redefining One's Own Self

Where do we begin in developing true feelings of self-value? There are four basic principles that help create the right attitude on which to build genuine self-worth:

1. **Take responsibility for redefining your own self.** This is a choice you make, and only you can make, for yourself. Come to grips with the truth that if you let others define you, you will live with destructive and unfounded conclusions because NO other person can truly see all of who you are or have only your best interests at heart.

2. **Choose to redefine yourself according to issues related to character, integrity, and reputation.** These are the aspects of a person that LAST. Surface issues are temporary, often fleeting.

3. **Stop turning to others for constant reinforcement.** Some people are crushed if they don't get affirmation, rewards, or compliments from other people. The best way to turn this around is to become a person who GIVES affirmation, rewards, and compliments. When you take your eyes off yourself and focus on what you can give to

others, you will likely find that others give back to you even more than you give! On the other hand, if you are constantly begging emotionally for the love and attention of others, you usually will find yourself disappointed.

4. **Recognize the difference between God-given traits and character.** Begin to place your primary focus on character.

God-given traits are not something we should boast about—these traits are a gift for us to use to help other people. A person may be musical, good-looking, intelligent, athletic, or any number of other things when it comes to inborn traits. These traits are of very little WORTH, however, unless they are developed and "given away" to help others.

Character, in contrast, is NOT something inherent. Character is something we must develop. In the end, it is our character that determines HOW and the EXTENT to which we use our inborn traits to help others! The inborn trait is not the deciding factor. Character traits are the deciding factors!

Let me give you an example. A person may not have much intelligence or talent, but let us assume that this person has developed good CHARACTER qualities. He shows up on time and puts in a hard and honest day's work. He obeys the law and keeps the rules of the workplace. He helps his co-workers whenever and in whatever ways he can. He serves others with a sense of honor and accountability. He does his best at the tasks he is assigned to do, and is willing to give extra effort and put in extra time. He works to develop the intelligence and talent he does have. What will your conclusion be?

That person is going to be well-respected, trusted, and admired! He is likely to be someone you want on your team.

But let's now assume that a person has a great deal of talent and intelligence. He does NOT, however, have good character qualities. He is lazy and does his work in a haphazard, inconsistent way. He is rude to his co-workers and sidesteps the rules of the workplace whenever possible. He has a sour attitude and does not take advice from his superiors. He is a reluctant worker, always finding fault with some thing or some person. He assumes that he is superior to others around him. What will your conclusion be? Probably that this is a person to be avoided! He surely won't have your respect, trust, or admiration.

What matters most? Intelligence, talent, personality, or social background? Or character? In the end, character always comes out on top.

## Develop an Area of Excellence

In addition to creating a new and stronger attitude on which to build self-worth, one of the most important things you can do is to discover and develop one or two areas in which you have or know you can achieve a high level of competence. This area may not be related to your career.

When I was in college I taught myself to play the guitar. I loved music and although music was totally irrelevant to my engineering classes or my career choice at the time, I felt good about being able to play the guitar well. That feeling translated into self-worth. It gave me a foundation for believing that I could learn and achieve just about anything I set my mind to doing and was willing to practice doing. I have seen this same thing happen in the lives of numerous people I know.

Are you a good cook?

Can you sing?

Do you have artistic talents?

Are you a great encourager or cheerleader of people?

Are you an accountable, resourceful, dependable, honest person?

Focus on what you do well. Focus on areas in which you have achieved. Focus on your strengths.

> **Every person has SOMETHING they do well. Find that area and build on it!**

Every person has SOMETHING they do well. Find that area and build on it! See yourself as a person capable of achieving, learning, performing, or doing!

You will also find that your own feelings of self-worth are greatly enhanced if you will:

- Continue to pursue a dream even when others around you are quitting.

- Motivate yourself to get moving and make small progress when you begin to feel twinges of self-doubt.

- Express respect to your peers for their success—they will mirror respect back to you.

- Overcome a fear—for example, a fear of public speaking or flying.

- Stop a bad habit, such as smoking or overeating.

- Solve a problem on your own.

- Do something well, even if it is just a small thing.

# Develop a Pattern of Positive Self-Talk

Positive self-talk can be tremendously beneficial as you develop your own feelings of self-worth. Let me make some very practical suggestions to you.

Write down three or four characteristics you aspire to, and read them daily as affirmations. You may want to put them on your bathroom mirror, the dashboard in the car, or on your computer monitor. The human mind operates on the GIGO principle: "Garbage in, garbage out." If you put fears, negative criticisms, or trash concepts into your mind, you'll get out fear, negativity, and trash beliefs about yourself! If you put in positive affirmations, you'll likely become more positive about yourself. Identify your assets and strengths, and focus on them every day. Say aloud to yourself:

- I am a person of integrity.

- I am loyal and dependable.

- I am persistent and resilient.

- I am sensitive and compassionate.

- I am decisive, optimistic, and creative.

- I am available and teachable.

If you need to work on certain areas in your life, learn to express those areas in a positive way:

- I am developing the ability to control my anger and jealousy.

- I am becoming more confident, decisive, and optimistic.

- I am a better husband and father every day.

- I am becoming a great encourager of people.

## A WARNING ABOUT POSITIVE SELF-TALK

Positive thinking and positive self-talk have a potential downside and I don't want to ignore it. If we try to convince ourselves that we are sufficient in and of ourselves we can fall into the trap of "self-worship." Any time a person thinks he is "numero uno"...the only "genius" in the room...or the most beautiful or irresistible person in the crowd...that person has crossed a line into arrogance and pride. Affirmations and positive self-talk are powerful and useful, so long as we don't begin to worship ourselves.

> **Affirmations and positive self-talk are powerful and useful, so long as we don't begin to worship ourselves.**

We are all limited in some way...and that's good cause for us to openly recognize that we need other people.

We all can do only so much...and that's good cause for us to rely on others for help.

We only have so many hours in a day...and that's good cause to be grateful for what we do have and can accomplish.

I personally believe that the best case for a positive and thankful self-image is this: We are created by a God who loves us and does not make mistakes. As one famous American artist once noted, "God don't make no junk!" This means to me that God should get the credit for what I become because He gave me the raw material to work with in the first place. He is also the One who has given me the time and opportunity to develop my inborn traits, good relationships, and character. I must acknowledge the truth that I did not create myself. I can only seek to develop what has been placed inside me.

Positive self-talk is useful in helping us focus our thinking on our potential for success and on the need to use our strengths to overcome weaknesses. It is never something that should be employed to convince ourselves that we are little "gods" or that we are in any way superior to others. If that occurs, we have done ourselves far more damage than good!

# Focus on the Three Gs

I recently learned a very powerful concept and exercise that can help any person build strong self-esteem. Every day as you awaken, focus on these three Gs:

1. **GOOD.** What are you GOOD at doing? Begin with one thing that you know you can do and are good at doing. It may be a very simple thing, but focus on that one thing at the beginning of your day.

2. **GRATEFUL.** For what are you GRATEFUL? Focus on at least one thing each day for which you are sincerely grateful. It may be your own good health, the love of a family member, a skill you have learned, a bad habit that you are well on your way to breaking, a positive relationship that is developing, or an opportunity that is unfolding before you.

3. **GOAL.** Identify a GOAL that you can accomplish during the coming day. Think of something that you are determined to finish or act upon during the day ahead.

By seeing yourself as good...you are more likely to give your best and do quality work.

By seeing yourself as grateful...you are more likely to reflect a heart of gratitude toward others and develop healthier, more forgiving relationships.

By seeing yourself with a goal…you are more likely to use your time and energy more wisely.

The person who does high-quality work, has good relationships, and is productive ends a day with feelings of self-worth!

# Protect Yourself from Negatives

You are always going to encounter people who will rain on your parade. Some of them may even be "well-intentioned" people who think it is their responsibility to do so! Life has its naysayers, self-appointed critics, experts, and name-callers. There will always be people who seem to know what's best for you. Sometimes even people who love us and think they are protecting us can say things that produce self-doubt in us: "You can't do that"…"You're not a leader"…"You've never done anything like that before"…"Remember the last time you tried something like that?"…and worse. Sometimes people very close to you can jeopardize your progress simply because they fear change, because their goals and values are different from yours, or because they are afraid they will "lose" their relationship with you if you become too successful.

I realized years ago that I needed to protect my mind from these "opinions" of others. I decided to become very careful about who and what I allowed to have influence over me. I began to ask myself three questions before I ever followed the advice of others:

- Have they done what I want to do?

- Do they have good, reliable, accurate information?

- Are their goals the same as mine, or as big?

Let's suppose for a moment that each of us has been given a glass of water that has been tainted to some degree with red food coloring.

The red color symbolizes the negatives we have experienced. Some glasses are darker red than others. Negative experiences seem to happen randomly and some people encounter more negative experiences than others.

How can we reduce the red color in our glass of water? By ADDING pure, fresh, uncolored water! If you pour enough fresh, clear water into the container, the red coloring can become so diluted that it is barely visible, and may even become so diluted that it is *invisible*.

Every person can, by his or her choices, change the "color" of his or her own self-perception.

Choose to run your own race with a positive self-image. Choose to be sustained by your own belief that you have what it takes to live a significant life. Choose to associate with others who will encourage and empower you along the way. Choose to believe that God has a plan for your life and that you can find it and follow it.

## Temporarily Borrow from Others

Often we become stuck in our own bad habits and self-limiting concepts. We know our weaknesses and hesitate to risk stepping into new areas. We may need a little push from someone who sees better things for us.

I am very blessed in having a unique wife and partner. From the beginning, Nancy was exactly what I needed. When we met in college, I was a small-thinking, rather negative, and seriously analytical engineer. I was ambitious and had a few hidden talents, but I was more focused on what I observed as the strengths in others rather than on the strengths inside myself. I had developed a confidence in my ability to master academic subjects, but not in my ability to succeed in leading people.

I had very little awareness of the great importance of character, the necessity of setting personal goals, or the importance of believing in myself. My self-beliefs limited me.

As an aeronautical engineer I knew I could function well in the narrow world of science and technology. But I had never succeeded in the world of business or leadership. I had not been an obvious leader in high school or college. At Purdue University all of my awards were for academic achievements, not for being captain of the football team or president of a fraternity.

When I realized that my career in aerospace was limiting, and that I wanted far more out of life than my bosses were anticipating for me, I knew I was facing a crisis. I needed to begin to believe I could succeed in a new area. I needed to become an entrepreneur, a leader, and an influencer of people. I even needed to develop an ability to speak before large groups...*gulp!*

My secret weapon was, and is, my wife. Her optimism, her decisiveness, and her unsubstantiated confidence in me were amazing. Nancy's perceived weakness was that she was not much into details, and she didn't really like to talk to people. But she was a great dreamer! She was an optimist and a person of action!

Nancy told me repeatedly that she believed I could do anything, including being successful in a people business. I thought she was crazy, and I often found myself scrambling to keep up with the goals she convinced me we could achieve together. She chose a unique strategy, which I now know included telling me I had done something well when, in fact, my performance had been rather pathetic. She believed that it was more important for me to believe in myself than to point out an imperfection. One of her mottos has always been, "It's better to praise them than to perfect them." As my confidence grew, so did my skill and effectiveness...which proved her right!

Do you remember George Bernard Shaw's classic tale of *Pygmalion* (also known as the award-winning musical *My Fair Lady*)? The sophisticated Professor Higgins bets his friend that he can transform a common flower vendor, Eliza Doolittle, into a lady. The theory is that people will become as you treat them. As Ms. Doolittle is treated like a lady and begins to speak like a lady, she becomes a lady.

> **It's better to praise them than to perfect them.**

Some parents and bosses are good at reinforcing the positive. They can often be heard saying, "You are always so good at that"…"I always expect good things from you"…"You are amazing when you do that." Other parents and bosses are good at reinforcing the negative: "You never do anything right." What we reinforce is what becomes the reality. Never allow another person to lower the ceiling of your success!

I responded to Nancy's POSITIVE reinforcement. I became who she always said I was!

## Begin the Process Today

My friend Charles "Tremendous" Jones has always said, "You will be the same today as you will be in five years, except for two things: the books you read and the people you meet."

Through the years I have read dozens of books aimed at transforming a person's attitudes and self-esteem. I have chosen to hang around only those people who contributed positively to my goals and beliefs. I have brushed myself off when I failed and made a determination, in the words of John Maxwell, to "fail forward." I have built a positive self-image by taking many small steps.

For me, six steps were vital and I share these principles with you:

**1. Borrow beliefs from those who believe in you.** Nancy was my "Professor Higgins." Someone once said, "I am not what I think I am...I am not what YOU think I am...I am what I think you think I am!" We become a reflection of how we are treated and perceived. Choose to borrow beliefs from those who believe in you and in what you can become. If you don't have an encourager in your life...find one!

> **I am not what I think I am...I am not what YOU think I am... I am what I think you think I am!**

**2. Choose books and recordings that promote positive self-worth.** Many classic self-help books are on the market from positive, accomplished people. Also listen to audio recordings and CDs that reveal how other people have successfully overcome fears, insecurities, and problems, or have developed positive attitudes and good skills.

**3. Make positive associations.** Get around people who are willing to believe in you and edify you, not tear you down. Rather than be in environments that encourage you to "compete" with others, get in groups that teach you how to "complete" others.

**4. Take success one step at a time.** I am a strong believer in baby steps. Even the smallest steps can result in accomplishment over time. Take life one day at a time and one step at a time.

**5. Begin to encourage yourself.** Stop the cycle and habit of telling yourself how inadequate you are. Begin to affirm your own goals and small successes. Speak to yourself the attributes of the person you WANT to become.

6. **Get an eternal perspective.** Remember that you are created by God and you are not a mistake. You are special and made for a purpose. Your unique qualities, strengths, and talents are part of a grand plan and no one else can fill your role. Your talents are God's gift to you…what you do with your talents is your gift back to God.

Through the years I began to adopt a very simple approach to my work:

We don't have to compete.

We don't have to compare.

We don't have to apologize.

We just need to accept and improve…one step and one day at a time.

# The More "Attractive" You

People always seem to want to be "attractive." They don't realize that the most attractive person is a person who truly has a good self-image from the inside out…is secure…and is encouraging to others. The healthier a person is emotionally, and the stronger the self-worth and character of a person, the more that person "attracts" others. He or she is like a magnet. People *want* to be around such a person.

Somewhere inside you is a chunk of sculptured gold. Break through the concrete of the poor self-image that you have allowed to encapsulate and seal off the real you! Release the beauty, potential, and significance of your own life!

**Attitude is everything.**

## THE SICK CHILD

I once heard a story about a professional golfer who was leaving the clubhouse one day after a major tournament win. He encountered a woman in the parking lot who shared with him that her baby was in the hospital. She had limited money and she asked the golfer if he could spare some of his winnings to help her seriously ill child. The man was very troubled by her story and wanted to help—so much so that he was moved to sign over the entire amount of his earnings so she could afford an operation to save her baby.

A day or two later, the golfer went back to the clubhouse and was sharing this story with some of the men there. Various ones said, "Oh, no! You have been tricked! This woman has done this before. We are so angry that you have become another of her victims. It is all a ruse so she can get money!"

The golfer replied, "You mean there is no sick baby?"

They said, "That's right!"

Then the man said, "That's the best news I've heard all week!"

When I first heard this story, I had to pause and let the message sink in. I wondered how I would have responded to the news that I had just given my money to a con artist. Would I have been "relieved" that my fears for a sick child were unfounded, or would I have focused on the money I had lost?

What a wonderful perspective this golfer had! What a great test of his ability to see the "good" in something! What an admirable set of priorities! I doubt that very many of us would have passed that test regarding our attitude.

# Where Is Your Focus?

As I noted earlier, our son Eric has had his share of challenges. He has had a total of thirty brain surgeries—eleven in the first year of his life—and multiple ongoing difficulties. Through it all, he has been a shining example of a positive attitude to our family. Eric focuses on what he CAN do, and on his blessings—never on his "disability." He has seizures, shunts (tubing from the brain to handle excess fluid), is confined to a power wheelchair, and has no ability to get in or out of bed without assistance. Even so, he lives a full and rewarding life, and he never complains. Amazing! He has been in and out of hospitals and doctors' offices all his life and yet he skis, travels, and raises money to help other "disabled" people.

We once asked Eric if he could think of something he'd like to change about his life if it were possible. He said he couldn't think of anything at all. I asked, "What about having the ability to walk?" He said, "Oh, I didn't think of that, but then I couldn't play Power Soccer or help the people I help now. Even worse, I'd have to go to the BACK of the lines at Disneyland!"

Eric accepts what is normal for him and moves on. He looks for the good in everything. He doesn't waste time, energy, his intelligence, or his great sense of humor complaining or wishing. Rather, he focuses on what is possible and practical.

John Maxwell tells a story about a little boy who passionately wanted to be a major league baseball player. Like many boys in America, he wanted to break the home run hitting record. One day he went to the backyard alone to practice his swing. He tossed the ball in the air, took a swing, and missed. "Strike one," he said to himself. Then he tossed a second ball and took a swing. Again, he missed. "Strike two," he called. Then, full of determination, he tossed the ball in the air again. And again, he swung and missed. "Strike three, you're OUT!" he exclaimed. Then he paused a second to realize what had happened and said, "Looks as if I'm going to be the world's greatest pitcher!"

This little boy, like Eric, adjusted his outlook but maintained his attitude as a winner. He was determined to find the positive in the midst of what other people might see as the negative. How are you at doing that?

## Is Attitude Something You Have from Birth?

Are some people born to be positive and optimistic, while others are not? I believe there are some inborn tendencies. I, for example, have a naturally "realistic" view of things. My wife calls it negativity and she is right on occasion. As a former engineer, I thought that being "positive" was a sign of limited intelligence. After all, some things are not all that great. I firmly believe that it is necessary for certain people, at certain times, to consider the worst-case scenario. For example, lawyers, surgeons, and even engineers testing something to see how it might fail during use, shouldn't just "hope for the best" and charge forward. They need to proceed with caution, eyes wide open and all options considered.

The reality is, people with optimism and a sense of expectation are rarely disappointed.

At the same time, I have come to know through experience and my own adjustment in attitude that having an attitude of expectation and optimism often makes things go better than they might otherwise. I have become increasingly impatient with worriers, pessimists, and naysayers who have an almost self-righteous approach to life—as if they alone are smart enough NOT to be optimistic or naïve. The reality is, people with optimism and a sense of expectation are rarely disappointed—they may not get ALL that they dream of achieving, but they achieve far more than those who never dream at all.

My wife, Nancy, on the other hand, tends to be inherently positive. She assumes the best. She expects things to work out. She is very intelligent, but she is a lot like the golfer in the story at the beginning of this chapter. She instinctively refuses to be a victim and looks for a silver lining in every problem situation.

Do you remember the donkey character named Eeyore in the Winnie the Pooh books? He forever points out problems and negatives. At the other end of the spectrum is Tigger, the forever-bouncing, always-assuming-the-best character that often comes to hilarious but unsuccessful conclusions. No one really wants to be Eeyore—he is depressing and uninspiring. But at the same time, not everybody wants to be Tigger because he often comes across as being foolish and unintelligent. Even so, the truth is: The Tiggers of this world end up far better off than the Eeyores. Even if things don't turn out exactly as they anticipate, they still feel good! The Eeyores of this world don't *ever* feel good.

# The Disease of Victim-itis

Our society seems to have become conditioned to look for someone to blame for all negative situations. We seem to have been taught by certain psychologists, educators, and politicians that nothing is ever really OUR fault. We are encouraged to blame our parents, boss, the government, relatives, a wife or husband, the children, political opponents, a former spouse, a mother-in-law, a bad neighbor, or SOMEBODY...and at times ANYBODY...for things that go wrong in our lives. Our litigious society seems bent on not only finding someone to blame, but someone who will PAY.

At times, of course, there are people who willfully harm others, or do so out of negligence and carelessness. At times, blame may be warranted. However, the degree to which we assign blame in our nation seems epidemic. I find this extremely counterproductive to both individuals and to society. Good leaders and successful people stay focused on the future and allow little time for feeling sorry for themselves or in assigning blame. They understand that assigning blame and exacting payment or other compensation are time-consuming, energy-depleting activities. Good leaders and successful people would rather spend their time and energy on creating a better future.

Rarely is it a fact that a person has failed to reach a goal or failed to succeed in life because he or she was someone else's "victim."

Certainly there are circumstances that are unfair in life...but a circumstance never fully dictates the degree to which a person can have significance! In some cases, it is a negative circumstance that becomes the catapult that launches a person toward significance.

We all have dealt with circumstances that we WISHED were different. We have all been in situations that we WISHED were different. Those circumstances and situations, past or present, do not need to hold us down or hold us back—in fact, they will only hold us down or hold us back if we choose to adopt a "victim" mindset!

In the beginning of our business, we had limited resources. Most of our initial contacts were wildly *unsuccessful*. Then we faced the challenges of raising a child with severe health problems, and those problems resulted in huge medical bills. Were Eric's health problems and the medical bills a challenge? Absolutely. But the real PROBLEM we experienced at that time in our lives was a problem with our own attitudes and responses to the challenges. Initially we were paralyzed by the problems we experienced. Then we began to focus on solutions...and the more we focused on solutions, the smaller the problems became and the sooner we overcame the challenges in our path.

On what specifically did we focus?

- We focused on the fact that we had been given an opportunity through our business to solve the financial needs we faced as a family.

- We focused on the fact that Eric was alive and had the potential to thrive.

- We focused on doing as much as we could to support the physicians and hospital who were caring for Eric, rather than sue for the missed diagnosis at his birth.

- We focused on the blessings of having a son and on the work that was before us.

In many ways, our great financial need drove us to turn what was a mediocre business at the time into a thriving business that might provide resources beyond our lifetime and over Eric's as well. The "problem" was actually a motivation toward a new set of goals. The circumstance in which we found ourselves became the catalyst for renewing our passion, vision, and dream.

If you get lemons...choose to make lemonade! Don't waste your time wringing your hands and saying, "Poor me." Don't spend your energy looking for someone to blame or bemoaning the fact that life isn't fair. Get up and get busy! Once you've made a good lemonade, find a way to market it and franchise it! Stay focused on what's ahead, not what's behind.

> **The circumstance in which we found ourselves became the catalyst for renewing our passion, vision, and dream.**

I love the little poem that has been circulated for years titled "Paradoxical Commandments." I offer it here as a great example of how to put life in perspective.

## PARADOXICAL COMMANDMENTS
### By Dr. Kent M. Keith

People are illogical, unreasonable, and self-centered.
*Love them anyway.*

If you do good, people will accuse you of selfish ulterior motives.
*Do good anyway.*

If you are successful, you win false friends and true enemies.
*Succeed anyway.*

The good you do today will be forgotten tomorrow.
*Do good anyway.*

Honesty and frankness make you vulnerable.
*Be honest and frank anyway.*

The biggest men and women with the biggest ideas
can be shot down by the smallest men and women
with the smallest minds.
*Think big anyway.*

People favor underdogs but follow only top dogs.
*Fight for a few underdogs anyway.*

What you spend years building may be destroyed overnight.
*Build anyway.*

People really need help, but may attack you if you
help them.
*Help people anyway.*

Give the world the best you have and you'll get
kicked in the teeth.
*Give the world the best you have anyway.*

---

# Circumstances Are Neutral

Your problem may not be your REAL problem! In most cases, the real problem lies inside you, not outside you—it lies in the attitude you develop toward a situation or circumstances. Your real problem exists if your attitude shackles you...paralyzes you...or diverts you from taking on the problem as a challenge to be conquered.

When you fall down...get up.

If you fall down again...get up again.

We are never really victims unless we allow ourselves to become ones in our attitude and perspective on life.

The secret to our ongoing success is NOT in what happens to us, but in how we RESPOND to what happens.

The golfer may have spent his money...but there was NO SICK CHILD! Look on the bright side of all that has happened and may be happening to you.

> **The secret to our ongoing success is NOT in what happens to us, but in how we RESPOND to what happens.**

**Bloom where you are planted.**

## THE BLANK WALL

Two men, both seriously ill, were in the same hospital room. One man was allowed to sit up in his bed for an hour each afternoon to help drain the fluid from his lungs. His bed was next to the room's only window. The other man had to spend all his time flat on his back in traction, and a half-wall between the beds kept him from seeing the window.

The men talked for hours on end. They spoke of their wives and families, their homes, their jobs, their involvement in military service, and where they had gone on vacation. Every afternoon, when the man in the bed by the window was allowed to sit up, he described to his roommate all the things he could see outside the window.

The man who had to lie flat on his back found that he began to live for those one-hour periods when his perspective was broadened and enlivened by all the activity and color of the outside world. The window overlooked a park with a lovely lake. Ducks and swans swam there, while children sailed model boats. Young lovers walked arm in arm among the flowers that were of every color of the rainbow. Grand old trees graced the lawn, and a fine view of the city skyline could be seen in the distance.

As the man who sat by the window described all this in exquisite detail, the man on the other side of the room would close his eyes and imagine the scenes. One warm afternoon the man by the window described a parade passing by. Although the other man couldn't hear the bands, he could see them in his mind's eye, along with the dancing clowns, the colorful floats, and the decorated horses and cars.

Days passed. The man who could not look out the window began to allow seeds of envy to develop. As much as he appreciated his roommate's descriptions, he began to wish that he could be the one with the view. He began to resent his roommate and eventually, he felt almost desperate in his desire to take his place by the window.

One morning the nurse came into the room to find the man by the window had died peacefully in his sleep. She sadly called for hospital attendants to remove the body.

As soon as it seemed appropriate, the other man asked if he might move to the bed next to the window. The nurse was happy to make the switch, and after making sure he was comfortable, she left him alone. Slowly and painfully, he propped himself up on one elbow to take his first look at the world outside the window. At last he would have the joy of seeing the park below and all its activity! He strained to turn and look out.

What he saw was a blank wall! He rang for the nurse and asked, "How could my roommate have seen all the things he described to me? Why would he tell me about so much beauty, and in such detail, when all that is actually visible outside this window is a wall of dirty old bricks?"

The nurse responded, "Oh, my...didn't you know? Your former roommate was blind. He couldn't even see the wall." Then she added, "Perhaps he just wanted to encourage you."

Have you ever felt some of the emotions that this story conveys?

Have you ever wanted to trade places with someone else to the point that you were filled with bitter envy? Have you ever been extremely disappointed—perhaps something you had thought would be wonderful turned out to be far less than wonderful? Have you ever been the recipient of a gift of encouragement—and failed to appreciate it at the time?

If you live a life obsessed with what others have, you very likely will miss out on the joy of receiving what others are trying to give you.

## Jealousy and Comparison

Thankfulness, or gratitude, is a quality that does not get much attention these days. Jealousy and a competitive spirit are far more frequently the norm portrayed in movies, media programs, and pop music. Winning is rarely presented as a win-win approach that benefits all involved—rather, winning nearly always is couched in a distorted, winner-takes-all view. If we can't win individually, we definitely want to be on a winning team—with the losing team in the dust at our feet!

Our preoccupation with winning can lead us to feeling very ungrateful or unthankful—and yes, intensely jealous—when we find ourselves on the losing side of life. If we are honest with ourselves, we must acknowledge that losing is an experience that everybody has at some point. Nobody wins ALL the time.

What we usually discover is that even when we move into the "win" column after an intense competition, the position in which we find ourselves does not bring automatic joy or peace. Why? Because we bring our same ol' jealous, competitive, unthankful attitudes with us. There's still another battle or competition ahead. There's still more to take, conquer, or win. There's still an enemy to defeat. A jealous heart is rarely satisfied—it always sees a new enemy, acquires a new target, internalizes a new fear or affront, and seeks to gain something "more."

A jealous heart can easily become a covetous or greedy heart.

Covetousness and greed are highly destructive emotions that often keep people from attaining their goals. Jealousy, covetousness, and greed always keep a person turning from one side to another to evaluate the competitors in their race, rather than focusing on the goal straight ahead. I do not think it is any accident that "thou shalt not covet" is among the Ten Commandments.

So many people today want what other people have—their spouse, their job, their recognition, their popularity or fame, their home, their position. Very often they want what they *think* the other people have on the *inside*—their happiness, their sense of purpose, their peace of mind, their feelings of love and comfort. The truth is, every situation has problems, every life has trouble, every relationship has difficulty, every opportunity has a tough challenge or problem at its core. For every positive aspect, there is nearly always a negative counterbalance. No one is spared all of life's problems.

**Choose to be thankful for what you *have*...right now...today.**

What is the approach we need to take? Choose to be thankful for what you *have*...right now...today.

Often, while driving long distances with my wife, Nancy, she will say out of the blue, "Aren't we thankful today that Eric is *not* in the hospital?" I always answer, "Yes, we are thankful—but never thankful enough."

We each are challenged to be thankful for today's "good things"—not looking at other people, and not wishing and hoping for something more or something better. A thankful heart puts a person into position to bloom and not wilt...to attract others rather than repel others...and to run with a clear focus toward a good goal.

## Circumstances Are... Just Circumstances!

I have had a number of opportunities to feel the sting of jealousy in my quest for success. In my early days as an entrepreneur, I saw other businesses growing much faster than mine. I was frustrated that many of my initial contacts—my extended family members and friends—were not supportive. They mostly said I was nuts to believe that what I was pursuing would work. I found myself thinking at times:

- Others seem to get more results.
- This seems easier for other people.
- Others seem to receive more help and support.
- Others seem to have more resources.
- The recognition always seems to go to others.

My wife and I drove all over the United States looking for someone who could catch our vision, and we received virtually no returns. Meanwhile, our competitors were thriving. I felt irritated and embarrassed. Then, when we finally did begin to get some results, we were still far behind others who had started their businesses at the same time we had. I hate to admit it now but there were moments when I found myself wishing that I had "better luck," more help, or different friends! A person who is jealous often seeks to shift blame or becomes angry at circumstances. I was jealous.

What are you thinking today? Do you find yourself saying, even to yourself:

- I wish I had THEIR contact list.

- I wish I had THEIR circle of friends.

- I wish I had THEIR personality.

- I wish I had THEIR mentor or leader.

- I wish I could have THEIR territory.

- I wish I could have THEIR spouse...or THEIR children (or their lack of children).

The truth is, none of these things holds you back. It's your attitude of jealousy and covetousness that is holding you back. Circumstances are neither good nor bad...they just are.

Consider the following tale:

A gentleman in the Middle East had only one truly valuable possession—a beautiful Arabian mare that everybody agreed was absolute perfection. The neighbors often stopped by to say how lucky this man was to have this one beautiful mare. The man himself didn't know whether owning the mare was a good thing or a bad thing...he just knew that he owned a lovely horse.

One night this horse broke out of the corral and when the man arose the next morning, he discovered

66

that his beautiful Arabian mare was gone. All the neighbors came by and said how terrible this was. The man himself didn't know whether this was a good thing or a bad thing...he just knew the mare was gone.

About a week-and-a-half later, the mare returned and brought seven beautiful Arabian stallions with her into her corral. These stallions were all smitten with her. Now the neighbors came by and told the man what wonderful luck he had. They said, "You not only have your mare back, you have seven beautiful stallions!" The man himself didn't know whether this was a good thing or a bad thing...he only knew that his mare was back and there were seven stallions in his corral.

While the man and his neighbors were looking over the horses in his corral, the son decided to break one of these stallions so the family might sell it. The stallion threw him and he broke his leg. The neighbors came by and said, "That's bad luck!" The man didn't know if the broken leg was a good thing or a bad thing...he only knew that his son had a broken leg.

About this time the king sent his top military men through the area and they immediately took all able-bodied young men off to war with them. This son could not go because he had a broken leg. The neighbors came over and told the man how lucky he was that his son didn't have to go to war. The man said, "I don't know if this is a good thing or a bad thing...all I know is that my son has a broken leg and didn't have to go with the army."

This little story could go on forever! The point is: You don't know the future and you don't know how any circumstances of your life might "play out" over time. Circumstances are not inherently, by their nature, good or bad. Life is a series of events and it's important that we understand that events are essentially neutral—it's the meaning we give to those events and the attitude we hold toward them that ultimately determine how we respond, and therefore, what course of action we might take.

My wife, Nancy, and I have faced many seemingly negative circumstances through the years. Were our early struggles bad...or were they the reason we were able to develop a certain "toughness" to deal with future challenges?

Was our early lack of money and insurance a bad state to be in...or was it just what we needed to work harder and develop better leadership skills?

I have seen my "worst" appointments lead to my best results, and my seemingly "best" meetings lead to nothing. Very few things in life are entirely predictable...and even fewer things in life determine the future.

Too often we ask about our circumstances, "Why me?"

The real question is this: "Why *not* me?"

Circumstances come and go. Bad times and good times come and go. As the saying goes, "Life HAPPENS."

We may have experienced tough times in the beginning of our business, but within three years after Eric's birth, we were out of debt (having paid more than $150,000 in outstanding medical bills). We were living in a large new home, driving new cars, and achieving a degree of financial success that we had hardly allowed ourselves to imagine in the days when we were facing a mountain of debt. In fact, we found ourselves earning an amount that put us in the top one percent of all Americans.

We suddenly were able to purchase the very best medical care for Eric, to travel with him and our other children, and to hire outside help for his care. Amazing! And the even more amazing fact to me was that nobody had to lose in order that we might win. The negatives we faced were not rooted in competition, and neither were the positives we came to experience. We had simply taken life as a package deal with both problems and rewards. We turned the "problems" into "reasons" to work harder, smarter, and with greater leadership skills.

I certainly would never have asked for the circumstances or experiences associated with Eric's birth...but as I look back, I believe his health problems are likely the single biggest reason we are enjoying the success we have today in our business. His need was something of a "wake-up call" to get us on track and moving forward. His health problems were just what we needed to ground our attitude in gratefulness and to remind us daily of our blessings and our vulnerability. His situation was just what we needed to make us realize that no circumstance automatically determines the future—what we DO, THINK, and BELIEVE in the midst of a circumstance today are what set us up for tomorrow.

> **What we DO, THINK, and BELIEVE in the midst of a circumstance today are what set us up for tomorrow.**

Did Eric's problems go away once we had our attitude squared away and began to move forward in our business? No. He had more brain surgeries, a spinal fusion surgery, and scores of ongoing complications in the years that followed. Nevertheless...we have ALWAYS been very grateful that Eric is our son, and we love him in the same way we love our other two children, Heather and David. Would we ever have surged ahead in business if Eric's health issues had not been such a challenge to us? Who knows? I do know that wallowing in jealousy or blaming circumstances for our failure would have led us nowhere!

# Run Your Own Race

We each must decide the race we want to run...and then choose to run it with all our energy, strength, perseverance, and an attitude of "I WILL run this race to the best of my ability, intelligence, and skill."

We each must come to the conclusion that no race is ever over until we quit running. It's only when we quit that we fail.

The Tour de France is probably the world's most difficult sporting challenge. In the world of competitive cycling it is the supreme test of strength and endurance. The race actually has twenty races that are cycled over twenty-two days. The course covers more than 2,000 miles across France, including cycling through high mountains before the final leg of the race brings the cyclists down the Champs-Élysées in Paris. The race requires tremendous mental and physical strength and endurance. In 2004, Lance Armstrong became the first and only man ever to win SIX straight titles as champion of the Tour de France.

Armstrong's story as an athlete began in Plano, Texas, where he was a top swimmer and tri-athlete in his teenage years. Cycling eventually captured his full attention. He began training for the Junior National Cycling Team even before he graduated from high school. Armstrong went on to win the U.S. Amateur Championship and that set him up for a professional cycling career. By 1993, as a member of the U.S. Cycling Team, he was ranked fifth in the world and all of the cycling experts seemed to think he was poised to win the Tour de France by 1996. Prior to this, the only American ever to win was Greg LeMond, who was a three-time champion.

As expectations built for the race in 1996, Armstrong began to experience blurred vision and to cough up blood. This sent him to a physician. Tests were run and in the end, this top athlete discovered that he had cancer. He not only had a massive tumor, but the cancer had spread to all parts of his body—his groin, abdomen, brain, and lungs. The cancer was far advanced and his physicians initially gave him very little chance of surviving any form of treatment. In his lungs alone, he had eleven masses, and some of them were the size of golf balls.

In 1996, Armstrong went to Indiana University Hospital where he underwent brain surgery followed by intense chemotherapy. He spent more than a year in great pain and uncertainty as he and his physicians confronted the cancer in every way they knew to fight it. Armstrong survived and amazingly, within a year, he was told he was cancer-free!

Then Armstrong made a remarkable decision: to rebuild his body and retrain for the Tour de France in 1999. To train a healthy body for this race is an awesome feat, but to train a body that has been ravaged by both widespread cancer and intensive chemotherapy is nearly impossible. Some speculated that he might not even be able to finish the 1999 race, and virtually nobody expected him to win it. But win he did! And not only that, he proceeded to do the "impossible"—he won the Tour de France the next five years in a row!

When Armstrong tells his story, he draws this conclusion: He never could have won the Tour de France unless he had been through the cancer! He explains to audiences that his body was so ravaged by disease and the treatment for it that he had no choice but to rebuild his body from the ground up. He began to develop a new kind of "leanness" of muscle and strength that even the youngest and fittest athletes in the world have difficulty matching. Many athletes, especially body builders, "tear down" muscle cells in order to rebuild them with stronger cells that have greater power and endurance. In Armstrong's case, he was able to build muscle cells without tearing down cells. The cancer and chemo had already done the "tearing down" work.

> **Lance Armstrong says that he never could have won the Tour de France unless he had been through the cancer!**

Often, during some of the agonizing long-hill climbs in the mountains, other riders could be seen standing up on their bicycles and barely moving forward. Armstrong would ride by them at ten to fourteen miles an hour...*sitting down!* Lance Armstrong today is a testament to the power of the human spirit that can conquer what most believe to be insurmountable odds.

Was cancer good or bad? Neither. It was just cancer. It became, however, the base for something great in the life of Lance Armstrong because he chose to overcome this disease with a renewed vision, focus, and determination. He didn't spend time "wishing" for a better circumstance. He didn't wallow in self-pity, discouragement, or depression. He didn't spend months feeling jealous of other cyclists who were free of disease. He simply accepted the challenge before him and set himself toward turning all negatives into positives.

Lance Armstrong cycles HIS race.

The challenge you face is to find YOUR race and pursue the running of it with all your heart, mind, and strength.

Don't try to be someone else.

Don't wish for another person's circumstances or attributes.

Don't compare yourself to others or allow jealousy to take root in you.

The bed by the window may not be a better bed after all! And even if it is, it's not YOUR bed. Look for the blessing where you are. Run your own race, trusting the outcome and timing to God. And...never, ever stop running!

**Focus on rewards, not obstacles.**

## THE GOLDFISH

Like many of my classmates in high school, I went on to college to obtain what I believed to be the education and skills necessary to have a life of success. I chose aeronautical engineering as my major. I was very interested in science and at the time, the U.S. space program was just beginning. When the Russians launched the first orbiting satellite called Sputnik, I felt inspired to see what I might contribute in the conquest of this new frontier called outer space. I chose to attend Purdue University because it had the largest and most respected school of aeronautical engineering in the nation at that time, and because it was the school of choice for the first nine American astronauts, including Neil Armstrong, who was the first man ever to walk on the moon.

I was excited to be enrolled in classes such as aerodynamics, thermodynamics, advanced calculus, and quantum physics. At the time, I assumed this was going to be my "life"—I envisioned acquiring lots of information, earning advanced degrees, landing a good job in a great company, and succeeding in life. I had absolutely no idea that one of the most important lessons I would ever learn during my time at Purdue would come from outside the classroom.

Like so many other insecure and enthusiastic young men arriving on the Purdue campus, I wanted to "fit in" to the social life. Since Purdue had about twenty-five thousand students at the time, the best avenue I could see for "fitting in" was to become a member of a social fraternity. You may have seen movies about frat houses; the image always seems to be one of a big house at the edge of a campus with lots of guys living the "good life." I was given an opportunity to join one of the best fraternities at Purdue, which came as quite a surprise to me. Many of the top athletes on campus were members and the guys seemed to be fun. I thought it would be smart to join the minute I was offered a place.

What I didn't know was that this particular fraternity had so many athletes with such poor grades that the house was on academic probation. The fraternity needed some members with good grades to keep the fraternity in good standing with the university. Since I was a straight-A student, I was a perfect candidate. Of course, I thought I was selected because the members of the house saw me as "cool." I had no clue.

The way a fraternity functions is that a person must first be a "pledge." Those who are full members of the fraternity usually make life quite difficult for the new recruits, often daring the pledge to pass various tests before he is rewarded with full membership. This testing part of the process lasted a few weeks as I recall, and I was very ready to do my part in enduring all sorts of humiliating challenges that were thrown at me. I finally came to the point where I was told of one final test I had to complete—and that was to swallow a live goldfish. That's right...*LIVE!*

I couldn't believe I was being asked to do such a thing! I had some real fears about whether I would be able to get that wiggly thing down, much less keep it down. I had lots of questions about whether that fish would continue to wiggle after I swallowed it, whether it would suffer, and what kind of impact it might have on my stomach. But, after all I had endured to get to that point, I wasn't about to quit.

I won't go into details...let it suffice to say that I passed the test. I wanted in. I thought the challenge was ridiculous but worth accomplishing. And at the time, it seemed I had no option. I HAD to overcome my initial misgivings and take the challenge.

Looking back, I see the silliness of the whole thing. But in that place at that time, in an environment in which fear was ridiculed and strength was rewarded, I felt I had no choice but to do what I had to do.

Was swallowing a live goldfish worth what I got—membership in the fraternity? Not really. Fraternity life tends to be way overrated. But the one good thing that did come from my being part of that fraternity was that one of my frat brothers introduced me to Nancy! When I look back after thirty-seven years of marriage to Nancy, I am glad I overcame all of my initial fears and misgivings and swallowed that goldfish!

But, you may be saying, what does swallowing a goldfish have to do with your later success in business?

Like so many things in life, every obstacle that is faced and overcome...every fear that is confronted and defeated...leads a person to a place and a level that the person would not have been able to reach otherwise. You can use virtually any experience that requires courage to further your own success.

# Fear Is Common to All People

Fear is an emotion that has been built into every person as a protection mechanism. You likely are familiar with the expression "flight or fight," which refers to the brain's automatic response to danger. When we perceive that our safety is threatened, we have an immediate instinct to either run or to stand and fight the oncoming threat. The threat to our safety doesn't even need to be *real*. Even a perceived or "believed" threat can trigger a flight-or-fight response.

At times, our fear is not related to a physical and external danger but to a fear that is much more internal—for example, a fear of failure or a fear of embarrassment. Such fears are not life-threatening, but we can have a strong emotional reaction to them nonetheless. We may find that our fear causes us to run away—emotionally if not literally—and to refuse to take a risk that has the potential to IMPROVE our life. We may find that our fear paralyzes us, so we take no action at all. We may find that we immediately respond with something of a "fight" response in which we lash out at those who are giving us the challenge, find all sorts of excuses for not pursuing the challenge, or blame all sorts of people or things for putting the challenge in our path in the first place.

People have all sorts of internal fears, including a fear of change, a fear of making a decision, a fear of taking on the responsibilities that are perceived to go with a promotion or a move to the next level in life, a fear of discomfort, or a fear of putting something at risk.

Years ago when I first launched my own business, I definitely knew that the potential existed for failure and subsequent embarrassment. Most of those who advised me at that time said bluntly, "This will never work." I especially had fears of talking to potential partners, which not only included the fear of speaking to them about my business but also the fear of being rejected by them personally. As an engineer I had been trained to use my brain within what seemed to be a rather safe world of scientific inquiry. Mathematical equations, scientific formulas, and computer programs are much more predictable than human beings! Starting my own business, although it was an exciting idea, was filled with unknowns. I found myself feeling fearful and hesitant.

Have you ever felt those feelings of fear and hesitancy at taking on a new challenge? I feel certain you have!

## What Are Your Goldfish?

What are you most afraid of today—not only in your business but in your life as a whole? What obstacles seem to stop you dead in your tracks?

Do you have difficulty:

- Setting a goal and committing yourself to accomplishing it?
- Forgiving someone who has hurt you?
- Humbling yourself to ask for help?
- Talking to people outside your close circle of family and friends?
- Overcoming what you perceive to be embarrassing moments?
- Asking forgiveness from someone you have offended or hurt?
- Letting go of unhealthy emotions such as anger or jealousy?

Every entrepreneur faces rather obvious obstacles in the start-up phase of a new business. A lack of financing, limited time, underdeveloped skills, fierce competition, and a lack of information are only a few of those obvious obstacles for most people. The far bigger obstacle, however, is FEAR.

Fear is often what causes a person to cancel an appointment, claiming that "something unavoidable has come up."

**Successful people are the people who are willing to overcome their initial fears and do the things that unsuccessful people are unwilling to do!**

Fear is often what causes a person to procrastinate, especially in activities such as cold-calling.

Fear is often what keeps a person from doing his best or giving his all.

My little experience downing a goldfish taught me a valuable lesson about life: Successful people don't quit when things get tough. Successful people are the people who are willing to overcome their initial fears and do the things that unsuccessful people are unwilling to do!

## Making a "Go" Decision

A decision to "GO" can put you beyond the obstacle of fear. This is one of the greatest lessons I learned from my goldfish experience. Once I made a firm decision—"I AM going to swallow this fish"—things actually got easier. I didn't hesitate another moment. I downed the fish!

I believe this is true for most people who are confronting most fears. Once you make a decision that you ARE going to move forward, past the fear, and on to the goal you envision...things will get easier. You will start asking different questions, such as: "How?";

"When?"; "What first?"; and "Who do we need and where do we find that person?" Questions such as these motivate a person to find answers.

When I decided to launch out into the international arena with my business, I faced a number of major obstacles. The fears associated with this leap into the "whole wide world" were a little different from the fears I faced when I initially began my business, but they were fears all the same. Could I overcome the legal questions involved in doing business in a number of

> Once I made
> a firm decision—
> "I AM going to swallow
> this fish"—
> things actually
> got easier.

nations? Could we handle the language differences? Did I have enough capital to build the infrastructure and inventories needed? Would the same techniques that had worked well for us in the United States be valid and effective in other cultures? Where would I find the staff to support this venture, and how could I coordinate the personnel in such a widespread company? Where would I find strong and talented leaders in the various nations?

All of these fears and unknowns caused me to hesitate for a while, but once I made the decision to "move forward," things actually got much easier. Fear stifles creativity and puts a person in an awkward, not-moving-forward-yet-not-moving-back position. A decision releases creativity and energy, and puts a person in a firm moving-forward-now position. That's a much stronger place to be!

## What Drives You?

Author Tony Robbins has taught for years that we are all driven and motivated by one of two things: the pursuit of pleasure or the avoidance of pain. That certainly was my case when I faced the challenge of swallowing a goldfish.

I was pursuing the "pleasure" that I thought was going to be mine as one of the campus insiders and a "brave person" who completed all the challenges the fraternity threw at me. I saw this as a ticket to a better social life and thought my membership in this special group of guys would improve my image. I was naïve, but nonetheless, I was pursuing the pleasure that I thought was just ahead.

When I decided to pursue the idea of starting my own business, I was partly pursuing the pleasures I perceived would be available to me as a business owner. I saw fewer restrictions in my future income and lifestyle. I also was attempting to outrun pain. I desperately wanted to get away from the negative and restrictive confines of the industry in which I found myself. The lifestyle I observed among my fellow engineers, who had been working for the corporation far longer than I, was not what I envisioned for myself or my family.

This pleasure-or-pain principle relates to all areas of life. For example, consider the person who is confronted with the fact that he or she is significantly overweight. Most people hate diets and there's lots of hesitation in starting one! We seem to think that we must deny ourselves all of the "good" foods for the rest of our lives, rather than adjust to the concept that we can have some of that delicious pizza and tempting dessert occasionally, just not every day. What motivates us, then, to finally move forward and begin a weight-loss plan?

Some people are motivated by pain. They are tired of feeling tired or of battling painful knees and backs. They may be weary of feeling the pain we call "frustration" because they can't get into some of their favorite clothes. They perhaps have had a negative, painful report from a physician, perhaps even a report accompanied by a firm "do this NOW" lecture. They may have had a bout with disease or a frightening incident with their heart.

Other people are motivated by the pleasure they believe they will experience when they have a slim physique and earn even greater admiration from other people. Some want the pleasure of getting into a new swimsuit or new suit size. Others want the pleasure that comes with having good energy, sufficient strength, and optimal health.

What's important is this: Recognize that all pain is not necessarily a bad thing. Some pain can motivate you forward toward a goal. Also recognize that not all pleasure is necessarily a good thing. Pleasure can make you lazy, stall the pursuit of a goal, or even make you give up a "higher goal."

## PLEASING METHODS OR PLEASING RESULTS?

> **Successful people are influenced by the desire for pleasing results. Failures are influenced by the desire for pleasing methods.**

In 1940, a man by the name of Albert E.N. Gray gave an address to a group of life insurance sales professionals. I came across this speech a number of years ago and found that it offered a fresh perspective that was highly motivating to me. The speech was titled "The Common Denominator of Success." Gray's premise was one I noted earlier: Successful people form habits and do things that unsuccessful people are unwilling to do. Gray said this in speaking about successful people:

> But if they don't like to do these things [that unsuccessful people won't do], then why do they do them? Because by doing the things they don't like to

do, they can accomplish the things they want to accomplish.

Successful people are influenced by the desire for pleasing results. Failures are influenced by the desire for pleasing methods, and are inclined to be satisfied with such results as can be obtained by doing the things they like to do.

Successful people have a purpose strong enough to make them form the habit of doing the things they don't like to do, in order to accomplish this purpose.

Gray then responded to a question, "But if I have a family to support, isn't that enough of a purpose?" He said:

No, it isn't. For the simple reason that...it is easier to adjust ourselves to the hardships of a poor living, than to adjust ourselves to the hardships of making a better one.

These are simple-but-profound truths, shared more than sixty years ago, well before the "self-help" or success industry emerged as we know it today. The secret of success lies in having a highly desired purpose.

When you have a sure purpose—a highly desired goal—you will be motivated to overcome fears and all other varieties of emotional pain. You will move beyond hesitation and into action!

Mark Twain once said this about courage: "Courage is resistance to fear, mastery of fear, not absence of fear." One of the first steps toward a successful and significant life is to accept fear as being a normal part of life that needs to be conquered. Focus on the reward that lies ahead, not the circumstance that generates fear.

Facing down a fear, and especially facing down a lifelong fear, can be a very liberating experience. Decide today:

- I WILL finish what I have started.

- I WILL press forward.

- I WILL take a new step toward my goal even though I don't have all the answers yet.

- I WILL be willing to step out into the unknown with courage and confidence because I am aiming at something that is important and highly desired.

Give thought to what you really WANT. Let that be the motivating force that moves you beyond fear and breaks the invisible barrier of hesitation. Once you make the decision that you WILL press forward...downing that goldfish won't be any trouble at all. In fact, you might even develop a taste for fish.

**Build and protect your reputation.**

## THE BOY WITH THE ICE CREAM

Lt was a scene straight out of a Norman Rockwell painting. A small boy came into a diner and sat down at the counter. He was eager to reward himself with an ice-cream sundae on a hot summer afternoon. He checked his pocket to see how much money he had saved for this treat. He found five quarters. As soon as he caught the attention of the busy waitress, he asked how much the ice cream with chocolate sauce would be. She answered, "One dollar and twenty-five cents."

A big frown came over the boy's face. He paused for a moment and then asked, "How much for just the ice cream without the chocolate sauce?"

"One dollar," the waitress said brusquely, trying to hurry the boy into deciding.

The boy thought for a moment and then said, "Just give me the ice cream only, please."

Moments later the waitress returned with the ice cream, along with the boy's bill. She began attending to her other customers. The boy finished his treat and headed for the cash register where he thanked the waitress and handed her four quarters for his ice cream.

When the lunch rush was over, the waitress returned to clean the place at the counter where the boy had been sitting. Next to his empty ice cream dish, she found a quarter left as a tip. She immediately realized that he had, indeed, had enough money for the chocolate sauce he had wanted...but not if he wanted to leave something for her.

To the boy, there was no option. He knew he couldn't use all the money for himself. He made a small sacrifice out of consideration for someone else. He was well on his way to establishing a "good reputation" that followed him throughout his life.

What a leadership lesson this is for us! The little boy knew instinctively what he should do. We all have an inner voice and a built-in sense of what "the better choice" is in most situations. The trouble many of us have is that we have also learned through the years too many rationalizations and justifications for not following that inner voice. We listen instead to a variety of competing ideas and emotions:

- I really deserve this little pleasure or reward...and I deserve it right now.

- No one will notice.

- I don't really know this person.

- I don't see how I can make any significant difference in this person's life.

- I don't agree with this unwritten rule so I'm going to ignore it.

- I'm having a bad day and I can't be bothered with the problems of another person right now.

- I think someone may just be trying to take advantage of me.

There's a well-known story about Sir Winston Churchill who once was walking down a street with a friend. The two men passed a "lady of the night." Sir Winston tipped his hat in greeting to the woman. His friend immediately admonished him for doing so, reminding him of the woman's reputation. Sir Winston replied to him, "Sir, I do not tip my hat because of who she is, I tip my hat because of who I am."

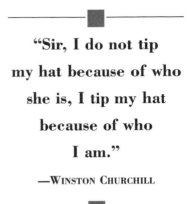

**"Sir, I do not tip my hat because of who she is, I tip my hat because of who I am."**

—**WINSTON CHURCHILL**

Our behavior gives rise to our reputation, and ultimately our reputation is a product of who we are and how we behave *even when nobody is watching*. Neither the little boy at the ice-cream counter or Sir Winston made a deliberate attempt to impress anybody. They were simply behaving in the way they knew to behave. They were choosing to do the "right thing" regardless of who might be watching.

Where does a reputation come from? It comes from what other people observe you doing when you don't know they are watching you. It comes from what others see you do as an unconscious, instinctive display of your inner values and beliefs. Who we are and what we do speaks louder than any words!

We all know people who "talk the talk" but don't "walk the walk." They have no authenticity as far as we are concerned. Their reputation is tarnished—not by doing wrong things, but by failing to follow through and do the right things.

Small acts of kindness and generosity—a daily example of putting another person first—are what build a solid reputation over time.

Small acts of selfishness and stinginess—a daily example of putting self first—also builds a reputation over time.

The question you must ask yourself is, "Which reputation do I want?"

---
**■**

**Who we are and what we do speaks louder than any words!**

**■**
---

## How Do You Want to Be Known?

Which of the terms below do you want other people to associate with you?

Why not pull out a pencil and circle the top three that you'd like people to use in defining you?

| | | | |
|---|---|---|---|
| Loyal | Selfish | Integrity | Competent |
| Cheap | Honest | Always late | Trustworthy |
| Dependable | Sloppy | Kind | Respectable |
| Courageous | Cheater | Generous | Resourceful |
| Prompt | Shiftless | Patient | Good follow-through |
| Selfless | Neat | Persistent | Sends mixed signals |
| Impatient | Arrogant | Passionate | Judgmental |
| Lazy | Scheming | Lukewarm | Tolerant |

First, define yourself. Then act to "live out" your own definition!

There are several different scenarios that the little boy at the ice cream counter COULD have followed.

1. The little boy could have ignored the waitress altogether and spent all his money on the sundae he wanted. This might

not have meant anything to the waitress at the time, but it would have meant something to the little boy. He would have taken just one more step toward a life based upon a principle of "enjoy things and use people" instead of "use things and enjoy people." In ignoring the waitress, he would have been totally self-focused. Over time and extended to its full logical conclusion, that approach might lead him to ignore the needs of others at all times, and become solely focused on what he wanted.

2. The little boy could have said to the waitress, "I can afford to have the chocolate sauce if you don't mind going without a tip." The waitress might have said, "Okay," and might even have thought his statement was cute. What would this approach have fostered in the little boy? A manipulative attitude. He may have been on his way to assuming that all people could be "conned" into doing his bidding if he simply couched his requests in a way that put the full burden of doing what was right on THEM.

3. The little boy could have tried to bargain, "Give me only ten cents' worth of chocolate sauce and I'll leave you a fifteen-cent tip." The waitress may have agreed but probably would have laughed and said, "Nice try, but I can't do that." What might this approach have fostered in the little boy? An attitude that shortcuts are possible and people can be used to give you a PORTION of what you want without your doing your part or pulling your fair share of the load.

The little boy took the path of generosity, with a straightforward attitude and no manipulation. I would like to have met the person who modeled or taught this behavior to the little boy. I have a hunch it was a parent or teacher who never even knew that little eyes were watching what he did.

# Your Credibility Is Being Tested

Whether you know it or not, your credibility and reputation are being tested every day in countless ways. Not all of your actions are going to be observed by others...but many of them will be.

> **Whether you know it or not, your credibility and reputation are being tested every day in countless ways.**

Think of three people with whom you work. In all likelihood, you can describe the character and reputation of each person with a few simple adjectives. You have come to some conclusions about the person based on the behavior you have observed.

Now think about how you feel toward each of these people.

Do you like working with each person? If so, why so?

Would you recommend a friendship, a partnership, or a working relationship with each person? If not, why not?

Keep in mind that if you can evaluate other people in these ways...other people are evaluating YOU in these ways!

When a company looks for a person to promote, or for a person to trust with added responsibility, that company usually looks at qualities other than technical skill or experience. It looks for a person who has demonstrated qualities of accountability, integrity, loyalty, and a team spirit. As an owner of companies that have hundreds of employees, I recognize how valuable a reputation can be in determining who to put in charge and how much to entrust to a person. A solid reputation of competency and trustworthiness carries great weight with me!

Every time you are observed acting in an honorable way—and especially so if no one SEEMS to be watching—you are making a deposit into your "reputation bank." This is one area in which you will want to generate as large a balance as you can! In fact, you will want to make huge deposits and no withdrawals.

However, should you find down the road that a situation arises in which something you do is called into question, a withdrawal may need to be made. For example, if you have established a reputation for being an honest person, you likely will find that others give you the benefit of the doubt should a suspicious situation arise. If questions are raised about something you have done that might appear dishonest, very often it will not be the words you speak in your defense that save you, but rather the reputation you have already established.

We often hear the phrase, "Your reputation precedes you." That can be good or bad! Having a strong and solid reputation for honesty, responsibility, and loyalty can pave the way to even greater success.

## Don't Seek to Be Perfect—Be Authentic!

Every person I know likes to work with people who don't need to be watched every second until a task is finished. One of the reasons I love to play golf is because golf is the only sport I know in which people call fouls or faults on themselves. For example, if a golfer touches the ball, or accidentally moves it, a stroke is taken. Even if no one else is watching, a true professional—or anyone who respects the game and himself—will report the fault and add a stroke. There are many famous stories about tournaments in which major money was lost because a golfer reported his own error when no one else saw it. There is great dignity in that!

One of the greatest stories I know to illustrate this is a story about Bobby Jones. He had a legendary reputation for honesty. He was one of the greatest golfers in history but he remained an amateur because he didn't want to spoil his love for golf with money worries.

On one occasion Jones was in a major tournament and he found himself in a situation where his ball was lying on leaves just off the fairway. The match was very close and a great deal of prestige was at stake. As Jones approached the ball, the official scorers stood nearby, along with several reporters. Jones was a strong favorite with the fans. As he prepared to swing, his foot touched a small twig and it, in turn, caused the leaves to move...which, in turn, made his ball "wiggle" just a bit. This was a disaster! It meant a one-stroke penalty.

**What is a win worth? Not nearly as much as a good reputation!**

The reporters and scorers let out a very quiet gasp as they realized this very small movement of the ball might cost Jones the tournament victory.

Then someone piped up, "I didn't see anything move, did you?" Another person quickly added, "I didn't see anything either."

Before long, all those standing by were trying to "help" Jones because they thought it unfair to have him lose the tournament over such an unfortunate and minor technicality. Jones, however, looked up and said, "I saw it move." The penalty was scored, and indeed, Jones lost by one stroke.

What is a win worth? Not nearly as much as a good reputation!

Not all golfers have such integrity, of course. There are also golfers who are always looking for ways to shave a point or two off their score. They may give the ball a small push out of the line of a tree, or drop a new ball where one was "lost," claiming the new one as the original and avoiding a penalty.

Through the years, I have found it interesting to play golf with potential employees or business associates. I have found this to be an excellent way to learn a great deal about their code of ethics and their character. Those who take shortcuts in their game are very often people who take shortcuts in other areas of their life. Those who openly and quickly admit faults and fouls are likely to be just that honest in their business dealings. Who would YOU rather have on your business team—the person who is forever scheming to his advantage or the person who is willing to own up to errors?

Let me share just one more golf story. It's about one of the greatest athletes of our time, Jack Nicklaus.

During his career, Nicklaus won six Masters tournaments, five PGA championships, four U.S. Open tournaments, three British Open tournaments, and two U.S. Amateur championships. Nicklaus, however, not only had a reputation for being a winner, he had a reputation for being one of the "classiest guys" to ever walk a golf course.

How did he get that reputation? Let me share an incident that happened at Royal Birkdale, England, during the 1969 Ryder Cup Tournament. Nicklaus and Britain's Tony Jacklin were arguably the two best golfers in the world at that time. They were representing their respective nations and they found themselves with the score tied on the eighteenth hole.

Nicklaus needed a win for America to retain the Cup, and the weight of England was on Jacklin's shoulders. Nicklaus was about four feet away from the hole for a par and Jacklin was just two feet from the hole. Nicklaus then did something that is still talked about today as "the concession." After he lined up and confidently sank his putt, he shocked the world as he immediately bent over and picked up his opponent's marker. He said as he did this, "I don't think you would have missed that putt, but under these circumstances I would never give you the opportunity."

The final score was an automatic tie, the first in Ryder Cup history. It was a moment of unparalleled sportsmanship that is still talked about.

The friendship between Nicklaus and Jacklin continues. Just recently they completed the construction of a world-class golf resort in Sarasota, Florida...together. The resort is known as "The Concession." Jacklin will live in this private gated community and in so doing, he and Nicklaus are perpetuating the spirit of that one gesture so many years ago.

What Nicklaus did was not necessary or expected...but it was classy. It was generous. He spared his friend and fellow champion any opportunity for embarrassment. He settled for a tie but in so doing, built a reputation as a person of quality and humility. Very few people would remember today who won the Ryder Cup in 1969, or even who competed. But we are remembering today what Nicklaus did on the eighteenth hole.

> **So much can be accomplished if you don't care who gets the credit!**

Seek to be an authentic person...not necessarily a perfect one.

Seek to be a person who doesn't continually look for credit or reward...you may find that you win the reward of a good reputation in the process.

Seek to be a person who has a solid reputation for the highest character qualities...you will be a sought-after friend, neighbor, and business associate.

So much can be accomplished if you don't care who gets the credit!

**Your past is not your future.**

## THE STARVING FISH

A number of years ago a powerful scientific experiment was conducted. I first learned of this through an educational film that featured Dr. Eden Ryl, a behavioral psychologist and speaker. In the experiment, a large great northern pike was placed in an aquarium and was allowed to feed on small minnows. Cameras recorded the actions of the fish over a period of days.

After some time passed, the scientists changed the conditions by placing a glass barrier between the large fish and all the minnows. Each time the pike attempted to eat a minnow, it was obstructed by the glass partition. After repeated failures and some pain from bumping into the glass and receiving no food as a reward, the fish stopped trying to attack the minnows on the other side of the partition. When it was determined that the fish was extremely hungry, the scientists removed the glass barrier and allowed the minnows to swim freely around the tank. They were fully available as food for the very hungry and much larger fish.

To everyone's surprise, the pike did not make any attempt to eat the minnows. The pike was swimming in a tank literally full of food—and it was hungry to the point of desperation. Yet it did not TRY to eat the minnows. After so many unsuccessful and painful attempts to get the food, the fish apparently was convinced that it should no longer TRY. The fish died...it died from starvation in a tank full of food!

Food was not unattainable.

The fish BELIEVED food was unattainable.

How many people today are in a similar position? They remember painful attempts at success, past failures, the embarrassment of a missed goal, and times of rejection and discouragement...and they form a belief that success and significance are UNATTAINABLE.

Our failure to continue to believe that we can succeed may not cost us our life, as in the case of this fish, but it could be costing us the QUALITY of life we desire.

## Making the Decision to Try Again

Ask yourself today, "What might I accomplish if I could begin today with no negatives from the past, no previous failures, and no painful memories?"

The truth is that you cannot completely wipe the slate clean when it comes to what happened in your past. But an equal truth is this: You CAN wipe the slate clean in the way you THINK about the negatives in your past.

People often say, "I've tried that once before and I don't want to go through it again." In all likelihood, you WON'T go through it again—at least not in the way you went through it before!

The world changes...and so can you.

What was true before...may no longer be true.

You can choose to get better, and in many ways, you may already have acquired additional skills or information that make you "better" suited for the challenge. You can choose to try again. You can choose to make adjustments in the way you approach a challenge. What was...isn't necessarily what IS.

In sports, such as baseball, even the very best hitters only record a "success" about a third of the time. The ones with the most home runs are usually the ones who also have the most strikeouts.

In the case of Thomas Edison, more than ten thousand attempts at inventing the light bulb failed before he experienced success. After each failure, Edison concluded, "That's one more way this won't work"—and then he tried a new approach.

The world doesn't need more quitters. It needs more people who will get up and go again. Rich DeVos, founder of the Alticor family of companies and a billionaire, once was asked, "What do you do when you get down?" DeVos replied, "I get up!" Sometimes it's just that simple. Going through a disappointment or a failure can be tough, but failures and disappointments are USUALLY one factor along the road to any genuine success.

This principle of try-and-try-again not only applies to business ventures and the completion of various tasks or projects; it can also apply to relationships.

Have you ever experienced a relationship failure? Perhaps a breakup or a divorce? Sometimes people become so hurt, and the feelings of rejection are so intense, they conclude that all relationships in the future will one day end the same way, and therefore, they refuse to give a new relationship a try. So many people say, "I will never trust another man (or woman) again! I don't want to ever go through this pain again!" Well...the past is not the future. Choose to learn what you can from the failed relationship and then recognize that every relationship is different. Recognize, too, that the broken relationship may turn out to be a blessing in disguise—you may have been spared even greater pain down the line.

If there's wisdom and experience to gain...gain it.

If there's forgiveness to be given...give it.

If there's a problem in your own life that you need to address...address it. And then:

- Get better, not bitter.

- Get stronger, not more fragile.

- Get wiser, not more cynical.

# Three Major Lessons to Learn

There are three things that every person is wise to learn earlier rather than later:

## 1. LEARN TO HANDLE CRITICISM AND REJECTION.

Don't wear your heart on your sleeve. If your boss doesn't accept your idea, turns down your proposal, or even openly speaks in a negative way about your performance, refuse to wallow in pain and self-pity. Ask yourself, "What can I learn from this? What do I need to change? How do I need to respond so that I can turn this around? Is there something in my idea, my proposal, my attitude, or my performance that I need to improve or adjust?" Start focusing on what CAN be done rather than on the emotional pain of the moment. Face up to the reality that every person is criticized from time to time, even the most powerful, influential, famous, and wealthy people of the world! Nobody is praised, loved, or accepted at all times by all people. That's life.

## 2. LEARN TO HANDLE EMBARRASSMENT.

Most of the time people are embarrassed by things that nobody else even notices, or remembers beyond the moment! People are simply too busy worrying about their own problems and failures to notice yours. I meet far too many people who are worried continually about what others think, and not nearly enough about what they are learning, creating, and doing.

> **Charlie "Tremendous" Jones says that too many people have "thin skin, and a hard heart."**

Charlie "Tremendous" Jones says that too many people have "thin skin, and a hard heart," when what they need to develop is "thick skin, and a soft heart."

## 3. LEARN TO HANDLE SETBACKS.

Failures and mistakes go with the territory of learning and growing. How many times did you stand up and fall as a toddler before you learned to walk? How many times did you fall off a bicycle before you learned to ride it well?

Take a look at any corporate growth chart. It rarely has a straight line going up—rather, the line is jagged, with periodic "down" periods. The overall trend is what matters, not one or two specific failures. Growth and success rarely follow a linear path.

When I started my business, I was pretty ineffective for many months. I tried to build a team, but my people skills were crude. I meant well, but I was very "green" when it came to my skills. I liked people, but my communication ability was poor. My engineer personality was good with computers, equations, and technical reports, but I was overly logical and sterile when it came to "people matters." My wife, Nancy, says that I needed to rent a personality just to conduct my first presentation.

I became discouraged and frustrated when I saw that, in spite of my hard work, sacrifices of time, and my total depletion of limited resources into the business, I wasn't doing as well as I had hoped. One day I asked a friend for encouragement and advice. I told him about our financial challenges and our lack of progress toward our goals. He attempted to offer some perspective from his own experience but he really had no solutions to offer me. He finally said, "Cheer up! Things could be worse."

I tried to cheer up and put on a happier demeanor...but within a few weeks, things DID get worse! Eric was born and all of the problems of our past seemed mild by comparison to his health problems. We would gladly have traded in the new problems for the old ones.

As the months unrolled over the next two years, we came to a very stark realization: We needed to draw a line in the sand and say, "The past is past. The future is ahead." We needed to start over, and starting over in our THINKING was the first step.

We needed to begin to believe that future results were going to be better than past results.

We needed to set new goals and adopt some new tactics.

We needed to pursue the challenge in front of us with a new commitment and new energy.

In reality, not much was different about the business that we were in or the business environment in which we worked. But WE were different. And because we were different, the results we achieved were different.

In the next three years, our little business grew to ten times its original size with ten times the income. We paid our debts, built a team, and, rather humorously, gained a reputation for being "fast builders."

There are countless people who have lived, worked, or performed in relative obscurity before they became an "overnight success." There are countless people who failed repeatedly before they suddenly emerged "out of nowhere." You can be among that number!

> **There are countless people who failed repeatedly before they suddenly emerged "out of nowhere."**

Have you ever heard the story of the Chinese bamboo tree? It grows rather uniquely. After it is planted and takes root, a farmer must water and fertilize that tree for five to six years with no visible sign of growth! Then an amazing thing happens. The tree suddenly begins to grow and within six weeks or so, it can be eighty feet high!

What is happening during those five to six years? The bamboo tree is putting down deep, deep roots that are capable of sustaining the sudden surge of growth above the surface of the ground.

That's what happened to us. We needed to change on the inside—in the invisible realm of our own attitudes, ideas, perspective, beliefs, and approaches.

## Break the Ropes of "Impossibility"

There's tremendous power in what you believe. You perhaps have heard the opinion of Henry Ford:

> If you believe you can succeed...you are right.
> If you believe you cannot succeed...you are also right.

Everything we do is ultimately fueled by what we believe. The challenge is to base our beliefs on truth, not on emotions, fears, or incorrect observations. The fish in the aquarium came to a belief that was based upon an incorrect view of reality. That happens to a lot of people.

It also happens to some circus elephants. Incidents have been reported in which elephants died in circus fires because they did not try to break free from the very small ropes that linked them to very small stakes in the ground. Why? Because when the elephants were very young, their trainers tied them to very strong ropes and large stakes. They "learned" that it was impossible to break free. They came to associate the feeling of a little rope around one foot with an impossibility. They refused even to attempt to walk away or to pull the stakes from the ground, even when the ropes and stakes became smaller and smaller in comparison to their size.

Do you know the "ropes of impossibility" that are keeping you from moving forward toward your goals? Are they:

- False beliefs?

- Incorrect assumptions?

- Incomplete conclusions?

- Paralyzed emotions?

- Attitudes of discouragement and despair?

The fish didn't have food because he thought it was impossible to get to the minnows. The elephants didn't escape because they thought it was impossible to break free of the ropes with which they were tied.

The good news is that you aren't a fish or an elephant! You can think...you can reason...you can change...you can overcome your fears...you can adopt a new attitude...you can begin to believe and to try again! You do not need to be shackled or inhibited by "impossibilities" that are rooted only in what you believe.

**Your past does not need to be your future.**

Leadership and human achievement require faith that a new possibility always exists in spite of past disappointments or current circumstances.

Your past does not need to be your future.

**Don't let the "urgent" speak louder
than the "important."**

# THE THREE-DOLLAR
# LIGHT BULB

Near midnight on December 29, 1972, Eastern Airlines Flight 401 was on its normal approach to Miami airport. On board were one hundred and sixty-three passengers and a crew of thirteen. The approach appeared normal until the pilot attempted to lower the landing gear. An indicator light that signals the successful lowering of the landing gear failed to light up! Since the approach was directly over the Florida Everglades, there was virtually no light from the outside to visually check if the gear was up or down.

A quick decision needed to be made. Without confirmation that the gear was down and locked, a landing might be disastrous. The captain requested a "go-around" to give him time for a manual assessment.

The pilot and his crew knew that there were two possible reasons why the indicator light did not come on. One was that the landing gear was indeed not lowered and locked. The other was that the light bulb had burned out. The pilots began to converse and even pounded on and wiggled the indicator light to see if it would come on...no luck. They decided to replace the bulb to see if that made a difference. As they were focused on replacing the defective bulb, the autopilot was accidentally disengaged, which meant the plane was on manual operation. No one noticed that the plane was losing altitude. Suddenly, Flight 401 made a crash landing in the Everglades eighteen miles from the Miami airport!

Everyone in the cockpit had become so focused on a three-dollar light bulb...nobody remembered to fly the airplane!

That night ninety-six passengers and five crew members perished simply because the pilots lost sight of their priority. They were distracted by the "urgent" and forgot the "important"!

We are seldom faced with such dramatic consequences for failing to keep our eyes on our priorities, but we all at times are guilty of concerning ourselves with what is urgent—the crisis of the hour—to the point of neglecting what are truly our priorities.

# On a Lighter Note...

Some time ago Nancy and I were at Walt Disney World with our perfect little granddaughter, Ashley-Kate, and her mother, our daughter, Heather. My priority that day was to give Ashley-Kate a great, fun-filled experience and good memories with her grandfather.

Ashley-Kate was only three years old at the time, so we were looking for the rides and attractions that would be best for her—certainly not Space Mountain! We finally settled on a ride called "Buzz Lightyear," a ride based upon a character in the *Toy Story* movies.

This particular ride has cars that are equipped with "ray guns" similar in design to the one used by Buzz Lightyear. I got into one car with Ashley-Kate, and Nancy and Heather got in the car immediately behind us. Off we went into the dark-ride adventure. The walls we passed were filled with colorful targets and all sorts of funny creatures that we were supposed to shoot at. A score appeared on our digital dashboard to indicate how many targets we hit. Guys always seem to love to shoot things and I was into this immediately!

Suddenly our little car stopped. I have no idea why but suddenly we weren't moving. We were still able to turn the car, however, and to shoot targets with the ray gun. So we did! I showed Ashley-Kate how to turn the car while I shot at the targets. We were laughing and having fun. Nancy and Heather were doing the same behind us and we called out to each other the scores we were registering. Nancy and Heather were beating me by a huge number—*ouch!* My competitive juices began to flow. I began to try harder.

About that same time, Ashley-Kate became fascinated by how fast she was able to spin the little car around and around. The more I tried to hit targets, the more she moved the car...which meant, the more I missed targets! Nancy was getting a higher and higher score, and I was getting more and more competitive.

Right before I was about to tell my sweet granddaughter to "stop spinning the car"—I came to my senses. What in the world was I thinking? This was not a competition between me and Nancy. This was supposed to be fun for Ashley-Kate, and to her, spinning the car WAS fun! I momentarily had forgotten my priority in being at Disney World in the first place. I began to laugh at myself and just then, our car moved forward and we flew through the tunnels. I lost in scoring to the car behind me...*big time*. But my priority stayed intact. The photo of Ashley-Kate and me—which was made available on the way out for an unreasonable amount of additional money—showed us happy! That smile on Ashley-Kate's face was worth any sum. I was ready to ride the ride again.

The point? Always keep the main thing as the MAIN THING!

# Distractions and More Distractions

What is it that causes us to become distracted from our main priorities? Sometimes it's our emotions, especially fear, anger, or pride. Sometimes we are overcome by a surge of greed or jealousy. Sometimes we lose our correct focus. And sometimes we fail to recognize or to follow through on some of the basic principles we know to be true. Let me remind you of two of these principles:

1. **You must succeed personally before you can genuinely help others.** I fly a great deal in my business and personal life and I have nearly memorized all of the airline pre-flight announcements. One of those announcements is related to the use of oxygen masks. I feel certain you have heard it or one similar to it: "In the unlikely event of a loss of cabin pressure, the oxygen mask will drop down. Please place it over your face, pull the strap over your head, and breathe normally. Although the bag may not inflate, oxygen is flowing. If you are traveling with a child, always put on your own mask first, and then assist the child."

   At first, this announcement may seem self-centered, but the point is this: You can't save or help anyone close to you if you yourself are not conscious! Your priority is to stay alive and to be strong enough to help others. Putting your own mask on first is not selfish...it is smart. In the long run, both you and your child are better off.

At times, high achievers are criticized for being too selfish or too ambitious. The implication is that if they will slow down their own success rate, others will be better able to succeed. This is rarely the case! For one thing, there is no "limited pie" that needs to be divided up. One person's success doesn't subtract from another person's possibilities.

> **Putting your own mask on first is not selfish... it is smart. In the long run, both you and your child are better off.**

And for another thing, it is the achievers, the entrepreneurs, and the ambitious risk-takers who create all the other jobs! They are the ones who protect and serve the very people who criticize their success. They are in a position of saving themselves so they can help others.

2. **You must clearly define your priorities before you can pursue them successfully.** Even the most successful people sometimes fail to remind themselves of their own priorities. It's amazing how quickly we can lose sight of what we truly believe matters the most. At times we do indeed lose sight of the need to balance priorities.

Consider today the priorities of YOUR life. Write them down. Ask yourself two questions as you take a long, hard look at your own list of "The Most Important Things":

- Are these REALLY the most important priorities to me?
- Are my priorities in balance?

# Three Areas of Priority

Priorities tend to cluster in three areas: spiritual life, personal and family life, and business and professional life.

## 1. SPIRITUAL LIFE.

This area is highly personal for each person. I personally believe we are all spiritual beings first, and physical beings second. I believe that God has a unique plan for every life and I personally am very intent on following His plan and fulfilling His purpose for me. The Bible says that we are to love God with all of our heart, soul, and strength...and to love our neighbors as ourselves.[3] That seems to me a pretty good foundation for priorities. The Bible also says this: "Do not lay up for yourselves treasures on earth, where moth and rust will destroy, and where thieves break in and steal; but lay up for yourselves treasures in heaven where neither moth nor rust destroys and where thieves do not break in and steal. For where your treasure is, there your heart will be also."[4] Again, this makes sense to me and my belief in this concept impacts my priorities. As far as I am concerned, my ultimate priorities are spiritual priorities that are in line with what I understand to be my Creator's plan and purpose for me.

The longer I live, the more I am convinced of this. I have seen that when my spiritual priorities are my foremost priorities, and when those priorities are in line with the statements above, I have tremendous peace and happiness in my life.

Does this mean that I regard financial or physical disciplines and their rewards as being bad? No. I simply remind myself to seek FIRST the establishment of spiritual priorities, and the rest seems to fall into line. I believe God can and does bless those who have their priorities right.

## 2. PERSONAL AND FAMILY PRIORITIES.

This area includes your personal health and goals, as well as your family relationships. We are very unwise if we pursue material success at the expense of either our health or our family relationships.

I strongly believe that a person needs to get enough rest to stay alert and fight illness, get proper nutrition and exercise, and leave a little room on the schedule for relaxation and recreation.

I'm a firm believer in leaving a little "margin" in your life. Can you imagine what it would be like to try to read a book or magazine if the words went all the way from the very top of the page to the bottom, and all the way from the left-hand side of the page to the right-hand side? Imagine no pictures, no empty space, no relief for the eyes. Talk about eyestrain! Talk about difficulty in reading and a lowering of comprehension! That's what life is like, I believe, if every minute of life is fully scheduled. We need some room in our lives for dreaming...for thinking...for just enjoying the fullness of a good experience.

Your children and spouse need time with you just to BE with you. If you aren't married, you know that you need to spend time with close friends to provide a "people balance" to the tasks of your life. If you have children, you know that they need to spend time getting to know you as a person, not just as a provider.

## 3. BUSINESS AND PROFESSIONAL LIFE PRIORITIES.

This area is one in which we need to manage time, energy, and resources very tightly. Distractions are one hundred percent predictable! At least four different kinds of activities will compete for your attention:

- Non-urgent and unimportant

- Non-urgent but important
- Urgent but unimportant
- Urgent and important

Your goal, of course, is to handle those things that are IMPORTANT as your top priority.

Consider the full variety of activities that you face on any given day:

- Developing new business (prospecting, networking, referrals, following up on communication)
- Serving existing clients and employees, including writing thank-you notes
- Reading and responding to e-mail, voice mail, and written mail
- Reading and researching
- Writing memos, reports, speeches, proposals, and "game plans"
- Having meetings and appointments
- Listening to educational or inspirational recordings
- Mentoring and coaching others
- Dealing with administrative and financial matters
- Resolving problems or conflicts

Each of these needs must be subjected to the urgent-or-important test. As far as I am concerned, those activities that relate to the expanding of a business and serving those who are dependent on me are my two top priorities. I have found that a person can spend hours dealing with e-mail, attending meetings, and shuffling paper...and not have anything of value to show for his efforts. A person can get so caught up in "administrivia" that he forgets to fly the airplane!

In most business enterprises, a certain number of new accounts or sales must take place just to stay even, let alone grow the business. If existing business is not serviced well, you can expect to lose even good accounts. At the same time, a manager or entrepreneur nearly always needs to keep up-to-date on current facts, figures, and trends...spend time with peers...and deal with the "paperwork" details. Finding balance is a very personal challenge, regardless of your business or position. Above all, you need to find a balance that still allows you to fulfill your spiritual and personal/family priorities!

## Keep Reminding Yourself...

In the end, you not only need to set priorities, you need to live out those priorities. To do that, you will probably find it very helpful to do these three things:

- Read through your list of top priorities every day. Engrain them in your mind. Drive them deep into your attitude. Schedule them into your DAILY schedule.

- Agree with your family members, especially your spouse, about your family goals. Agree with your physician or workout coach about your personal health and fitness goals. Seek agreement with co-workers or partners about work goals. The more agreement you can have regarding the goals of your life, the easier it will be for you to maintain your priorities.

- Have a mentor, coach, or accountability partner. This might be a different person for each of the three main areas of your life, or it may be one person who knows the whole of your life. I strongly recommend that this NOT be your spouse, but rather, a trusted older-and-wiser friend who has walked further down the path you are walking. Check in with that person periodically. Listen to and heed their counsel.

And finally, choose to manage your own time and priorities rather than have others manage them for you. Choose to set your own agenda rather than be sucked into an endless treadmill of "crisis management." Make a decision that you will refuse to sacrifice the important in order to do the urgent.

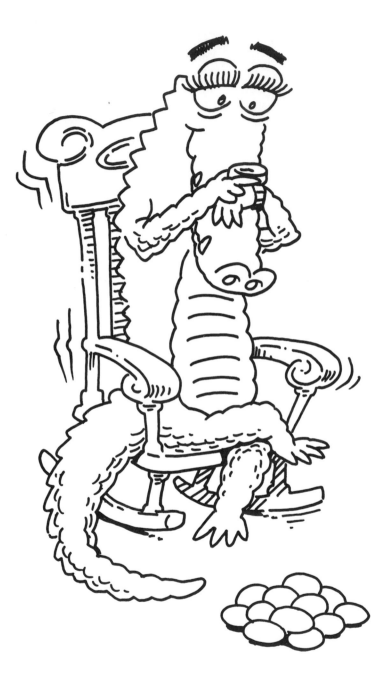

**Right actions at the right time.**

## THE ALLIGATOR

Y ou may not think that an alligator has anything to teach you about timing, sensitivity, or finesse. Prepare to make an adjustment in your thinking!

Unlike most reptiles, the female alligator has not finished her reproductive responsibilities the moment she lays her eggs. The real work of her life has just begun. A typical nest has twenty or so eggs. After laying them, the mother alligator covers the eggs with loose material to keep the eggs warm. Then she slips back into the water and remains close by to watch and protect her nest from predators. She repairs the nest as needed from time to time, and she can be quite aggressive if anything or anyone threatens the safety of her eggs.

Several weeks after laying her eggs, the mother alligator returns to the nest, tears apart the protective cover material, and, dealing with the eggs one at a time, she prepares to release her young from their eggshells. How does she know when to do this? She asks the eggs!

In the days leading up to this birthing time, the mother alligator returns periodically, uncovers one egg, lays her head alongside it, and gives a low grunting sound. If the egg "answers" her, she knows it is ready for hatching. If there is no "reply," she returns to the water and tries again later. Timing is critical!

If the mother alligator uncovers her nest too soon, the eggs lose their heat and protection and may fail to hatch at all. If she is too late, the little alligators may have cut themselves free on their own, but the heavy amount of vegetation covering the nest might suffocate them. The baby alligators must be released at precisely the right time and in the right way if they are to have a chance at life.

I'm not sure how mother alligators learned to deal with their young, but I suspect that over the centuries, they learned the hard way—by making mistakes and losing lots of baby alligators.

In your business, you don't want to lose good partners, good employees, or good customers, patients, or clients! Therefore, good leaders must always be concerned with two key ingredients associated with success:

- Focused listening
- Right timing

## Learn to Listen Closely

Most people who are leaders or high achievers are people who like to talk, always have something to say, and are in a position where they need to tell others what to do, at least to a certain extent. New or potential leaders, however, rarely see "listening" as an important part of their role.

You probably have heard the following statement or are at least familiar with the concept: "Better to remain quiet and be thought a fool, than to open your mouth and remove all doubt." There's much truth in this quip! Listening gives a leader an opportunity to:

- Give others an opportunity to provide you with important data or information.

- Give others an opportunity to vent emotions, which may impact working relationships and overall morale.

- Give others an opportunity to express creative or new ideas and insights.

There's tremendous value in listening!

I remember clearly the first time I read Dale Carnegie's book, *How to Win Friends and Influence People*. He made a statement that was extremely refreshing to me as an engineer trying to become an entrepreneur in a sales-driven business. I thought I had to become the best "talker" I knew in order to succeed. Carnegie said, however, "You can make more friends in two weeks by becoming sincerely interested in other people, than you will make in two years trying to get other people interested in you." I immediately turned my attention away from all attempts at becoming "interesting" and turned them toward ways in which I might show that I was genuinely "interested." The key to showing interest in others, I concluded, was to LISTEN.

> "You can make more friends in two weeks by becoming sincerely interested in other people, than you will make in two years trying to get other people interested in you."
>
> —DALE CARNEGIE

Any time you try to influence another person to buy your product or service, you are wise FIRST to:

- Get as much information as you can about the customer's needs or desires.

- Get insights into the customer's fears or doubts.

- Discover ways in which you might genuinely help the customer.

- Gain insights into the customer's ultimate goals and desires in life.

The only way I can get this information is by asking questions and listening closely to the answers I am given!

In my business today I spend a great deal of time and effort helping people establish goals and develop business plans to accomplish their goals. In many ways I function as a coach or consultant. Nobody is obligated to listen to me or to act on my advice—that's true in virtually every teacher-student, leader-follower, or coach-player relationship. I know that for a person to accept my advice, my advice needs to be perceived by the person as being:

- Helpful to their reaching a goal

- Accurate and pertinent to their life and needs

- Associated with something the person truly WANTS, and wants to the degree the person is willing to do some work or make some effort to get what he wants

The only way I can truly be effective as a coach or consultant is by giving advice that is PERCEIVED as valuable and doable. In order to give such advice, I need to ask good questions and listen closely to the answers I'm given!

When a leader interviews a person to come alongside him as an employee or partner, that leader needs to be very concerned about what the person wants in life...what the person is willing to give to the enterprise...what the person expects to receive from the association...and how the person regards the product or service involved. A leader needs to "ask the egg" before taking the next step of hiring or entering into a contractual agreement with the person. An interview needs to be mostly about listening, not about telling a future associate all the reasons he or she should become an associate.

Once again...the only way I can truly be effective as a person growing a business is to ask good questions and listen closely to the answers I'm given!

Periodically during a conversation or interview, I ask, "Based on the information you now have (or based on what you have just shared with me), what level of interest do you have in learning more?" Or, I might ask, "On a scale of one to ten, with ten being 'I'm ready to decide now,' and one being 'I'm not at all interested,' where are you right now?"

If the person gives me a number that's somewhere between one and ten, which is nearly always the case, I might say, "What can I provide you in the way of information to bring you closer to a ten?"

This practice sends a strong message: "I want to hear from you"..."I don't want to waste your time"..."I don't want to overstep your boundaries." The person on the other side of the table nearly always appreciates my willingness to listen to "where they are at" rather than barrel ahead with my own agenda and sales pitch.

## THE MESSAGE BEHIND THE MESSAGE

One of the things you will discover the more you practice your listening skills is that there nearly always is a message behind the message. People sometimes are reluctant to express true feelings out of fear that you will use their feelings to manipulate them. Others don't want to express true feelings because they don't want to offend or hurt you. Listen closely to what the person is telling you, and also to what they aren't telling you. Most people want to be "sold," not "told." They want to be led into making a quality decision, not prodded or nagged into making a decision. Be sensitive to signals that tell you the other person is willing to be "hatched" or needs to be left alone a while longer.

# Precision in Timing

We are a people and a culture in a hurry, but too often when we hurry to close a sale...rush to make a decision...or press with insistence to forge a deal...we end up with nothing. At the other end of the spectrum are those who are so afraid of getting a "no" that they never ask the question!

Being too insistent can result in damaged relationships and wasted time.

Being too hesitant can result in paralysis, procrastination, and no results.

Those who are overly insistent are often perceived as being aggressive, rude, insensitive, self-serving, and not at all interested in a win-win outcome. If your tendency is to push ahead for an answer or commitment, you are probably wise to back off a little and work more on building a relationship with the person.

Those who are overly hesitant are often perceived as being unsure, incompetent, or wishy-washy. If your tendency is to procrastinate or wait for the other person to take the initiative, you are probably wise to address issues of fear, lack of conviction, or lack of passion in your own life. Seek to discover what keeps you from being courageous enough to make definitive decisions or bring closure to a proposition. Recognize that people may be harmed by "default" if you fail to lead them toward a product, service, or commitment that is to their potential benefit.

Your challenge, of course, is to find a balance that's right for each relationship, each conversation, each sales call, each presentation, or each interview.

One of the things I've learned through the years is that influence comes only after trust is established. If a person presses for a decision before trust has been established, the response from the other person is nearly always negative. On the other hand, if a person establishes trust first and comes to a decision-making time later, there's a much higher probability that the decision will be one that works well for both people involved.

There are usually four questions all people ask internally before deciding to act on another person's request. These questions are valid not only in business relationships but in all other types of relationships—from dating relationships to coach-player relationships.

1. Do you care about me?

2. Can I trust you?

3. Do you know what you are talking about?

4. Are you committed?

If you attempt to gain influence, seek specific action, or close a deal before these questions are answered with a sure "YES" in the other person's mind, you likely will be unsuccessful.

You must learn to read people and project confidence, and at the same time yield to the other person's feelings and welfare. You must learn to find a balance between acting decisively and being sensitive.

Much of my business activity is directed toward finding ambitious people and then showing them how they can reach their goals. I meet a high percentage of people who know how to say the right things...*initially*. They are quick to express their goals, to convince me they are serious about their goals, and to get my advice on what to do. Then, when they realize that their goals aren't going to be achieved instantly, many of these people don't turn out to be nearly as "ready" to act as they appeared to be, or perhaps even as "ready" as they themselves thought they were!

The tendency of the seller in these cases is nearly always to tell a person too much too soon. If a seller (of a product, service, or business opportunity) finds an eager buyer, that seller is likely to dump a huge load of advice that the buyer isn't remotely capable of handling. I know far too many people who have brought up the possibility of a new business enterprise to a would-be associate and at the first sign of their interest in the venture, the person launched into a description of all the hours it takes to succeed, the discouragement that must be overcome, the changes the new venture will mean to their life, the investment of time and money that would probably be involved...and by that time, the would-be associate had already checked out and was no longer remotely interested!

Never try to turn a weekend athlete into an Olympics contender! A person may THINK he wants it all, but in truth, he doesn't know what he doesn't know and he isn't at all ready to make a commitment. It's a little like a man who has a good date with a woman and then suddenly at the end of the evening asks her to marry him. The woman may have enjoyed the evening as much as the guy did, but to jump to the level of a marriage proposal is to move way too far, way too fast!

Highly productive salespeople with a long track record of success know that many of their best clients are ones they took time to *cultivate*. Considerable time and effort was invested in getting to know the person and establishing trust. Sometimes the salesperson had to wait out the client until the client was unhappy about the product he was using, or perhaps until the product wore out. Sometimes the salesperson had to wait until the client wanted a significant change in his life.

Patience is not procrastination. Patience is a virtue. It is a steady, softly persistent presence that projects the message, "I'm here when you are ready to take the next step." Procrastination is NOT a virtue. Procrastination is rooted in fear and laziness.

Seek to develop a large number of sales-related relationships, each of which may be at a different stage. That way you can balance those relationships that are at a stage of "making a deal" with those that are at the stage of "first hearing about the possibility of a deal." Don't fail to act if a person is ready to act. Don't press a person who isn't ready to move forward.

Always seek to be sensitive to the WHOLE of what is happening in a person's life. At times a person may be facing a personal crisis and therefore, not be at all able or willing to entertain a business opportunity. If you fail to recognize, accommodate, or develop empathy for the non-business interests, relationships, and problems of a person's life, you are likely to appear selfish and insensitive. Try to find out as much as you can about a person without overstepping the boundaries of good manners and privacy.

All of these things need to be taken into consideration not only when "courting" a person to move to a more committed, more productive, or more solidified relationship. They also need to be taken into consideration if you must reprimand or correct a person.

Always couch your corrective measures with a dose of praise. I like the motto: Praise publicly and correct privately. Never violate a person's confidence or their ability to grow, change, and develop. At the same time, you are being helpful in the long run—not hurtful—if you will tell a person HOW he or she might be more efficient, effective, productive, or produce higher-quality work. Don't focus on the negatives, although you may need to be very specific in addressing them. Do focus on what the person can do to overcome, correct, or improve. Set a new standard. Help the person get their eyes on a new goal, a higher standard, or a more professional way of handling a problem or presentation.

> **The truth is:**
> **With the right timing, almost anything can be communicated in a positive way. With the wrong timing, almost nothing can be communicated in a way that it will be received well.**

The truth is: With the right timing, almost anything can be communicated in a positive way. With the wrong timing, almost nothing can be communicated in a way that it will be received well.

## Be Like the Mama Alligator

Have a sense of "protection" toward those you lead and influence. A good leader fiercely defends those he is leading.

Listen closely to those who are following you. Address their needs. Help them first to discover their potential and identify their dreams. Then help them pursue their potential and fulfill their dreams.

Monitor the growth and development of a person. Know when to encourage a person to move upward to the next level, and when to encourage a person to step back and get a new perspective or gain additional information and skills.

Every leader should have as a goal the raising up of a new generation of leaders who will take his place. In order to do that, you need to "listen to the eggs" and help people grow according to their own optimal timetable.

**Equip yourself for the journey.**

**THE HUMMINGBIRD**

The ruby-throated hummingbird is one of God's most amazing creatures. It is only three-and-a-half inches long but it has one of the greatest energy outputs of any warm-blooded animal. Twice each year this little creature travels from southern Canada to Panama! The trip includes one stretch that is about five hundred miles over water.

The typical sighting of one of these beautiful little birds is of it flitting from flower to flower, gathering nectar and insects. The hummingbird loses a great deal of body heat as it flies, and therefore it must continue to feed all day—as long as there is light—to replenish its energy and strength. Much of the bird's migration to the south each year is relatively easy, but then the day approaches when the bird is facing a long trip over nothing but open seas. This is no time to run out of energy!

The very night before the hummingbird leaves on this last and longest leg of its journey, it actually goes into a state of hibernation. Only about twenty percent of the normal fuel it needs for warmth is required in this state. The bird becomes so motionless that you can touch one and it will not respond. As soon as the sun begins to warm the air, the bird awakens and gathers some final nectar before heading out over the water for a five-hundred-mile flight.

I can hardly imagine a little creature only three inches long traveling that far without stopping. Almost needless to say, I am highly impressed with this bird's level of accomplishment!

We can learn much from the ruby-throated hummingbird about what is required in building a business or leading an organization. Certainly two of the key ingredients are ENERGY and PREPARATION.

# Keep Your Energy Level High

The hummingbird, of course, is not the only creature that spends most of a day acquiring "fuel" in order to stay alive. That is often the case in the animal kingdom. Humans may not need to forage for food every waking hour of the day, but human beings do need the proper nutrition for both their physical and their emotional life. Everywhere I travel these days I seem to encounter people who are low on physical energy and near exhaustion emotionally. Few people exercise regularly. Most people skip meals or live on fast-food and microwave-cooked dinners. Although this certainly is not a book on nutrition, I do want to offer you a few tips from my experience to help you boost your energy.

## 1. EAT RIGHT.

What does it mean to eat right? Mainly it means sticking to real foods, not processed and canned foods, or foods loaded with preservatives. Avoid fatty and fried foods, and yes, that includes French fries. Avoid additives and chemicals. Also avoid too much salt, white sugar, and white flour.

Our bodies are constantly being attacked by "free radicals"— these are substances that damage the body at the cellular level. Free radicals are increased greatly within the body if a person eats the wrong fats, smokes, or drinks excessive alcohol. To overcome free radicals, a person needs to eat lots of fresh vegetables and fruits, use mono-saturated oil such as olive oil on salads or in cooking, and eat only lean meat, fish, or poultry.

If you don't know the basics of good nutrition, I encourage you to make it a priority to LEARN what is good for your body and what isn't. After all, it's the only body you are going to have!

## 2. EAT LESS.

Obesity is a major health epidemic in our world, not only in the United States but in many other nations that are moving more and more toward a "westernized" diet. More than sixty percent of all Americans—and seventy-five to eighty percent of all adult Americans—are overweight.

Obesity is responsible for as many deaths and chronic health-related diseases and ailments as smoking or alcohol. How tragic and ironic that the most developed nations in the world are dying from too much food while the rest of the world is dying from too little!

The healthy way to eat is to eat smaller amounts and to eat more often. Protein snacking can be very helpful in regulating blood-sugar levels. By all means, you should avoid snacks that are high in processed carbohydrates, sugar, and hydrogenated or partially hydrogenated fats. Check the labels of any packaged foods you eat!

I don't at all recommend that people "go hungry"...just "go healthy."

## 3. EXERCISE MORE.

Studies show that only about fifteen percent of Americans have a regular exercise program as a habit in their lives. Gyms and health clubs make large amounts of money selling huge numbers of memberships to people who statistically won't ever come into the gym after a few visits.

I don't encourage people to become body builders or marathon runners. That degree of "fitness" is impractical for most people owing to age or physical and health limitations. What I do encourage people to do is to make a commitment to "move around more."

One way to do this is to count your steps each day. A pedometer that keeps track of steps can be very inexpensive. Walk the stairs, park the car a bit farther from the entrance to the building, do a thirty-minute walk or treadmill session three or four times a week. More is better—say, thirty minutes five to six times a week—but it is not required for significant benefit to occur. Cut down on sedentary activities such as watching television, surfing the Internet on your computer, or sitting on the sofa watching DVDs or videos.

Recognize that the more you exercise, watch your blood-sugar levels, and build muscle, the faster your metabolism will become and therefore, the more you will be able to eat without gaining weight.

## 4. USE SUPPLEMENTS.

The latest medical studies are very clear on this point: You are wise to add supplements to your food intake. Supplementation can really make a difference in your energy level, as well as help prevent or even possibly reverse many of the most serious lifestyle-related diseases such as cancer, heart disease, diabetes, and osteoporosis. Be sure to find the right source for the supplements you take—find a company that uses natural ingredients, proper manufacturing techniques, has good quality controls in place, and has safe-tested its ingredients.

You need to do your own research on what you should take and in what quantities. I suggest a quality multivitamin and mineral supplement as a base. Then I personally add a good balance of antioxidant vitamins such as C, E, and multi-carotene. Most people don't get sufficient amounts of the "essential fatty acids" (EFA). These nutrients are found primarily in fish such as salmon and in sources such as flaxseed oil. Supplements in capsule form are available.

There are many other very fine supplements and I take a number of additional things to push back my chances of disease—including glucosamine, CoQ10, a balanced B-complex formula, saw palmetto, and digestive enzymes.

Always remember that your cells are composed of what you eat. I personally would rather have vitamin-enriched, trans-fat-free cells...than to have French-fried cells that have been doused with artificial chemicals!

## 5. DRINK WATER.

A very high percentage of your body is water. Water keeps the cells hydrated and it flushes the body of toxins—both of which are important factors related to overall health. It is important to drink at least eighty ounces of fresh pure water every day, and more if you are exercising. Let me emphasize these words about water: *fresh* and *pure!*

I suggest you do a little research into the frightening amount of chemicals and additives that are in regular tap water. Carcinogens (cancer-causing toxins), industrial pollutants, and microorganism bacteria are everywhere, and they are rarely if ever filtered. Even commercially bottled water has little or no real removal of some of the most dangerous chemicals. Having a quality filter system is the best choice for most people—and cheaper in the long run than poor health.

## 6. AVOID SMOKING AND DRINKING ALCOHOL.

This is always a sensitive subject because some people feel very strongly about these substances. I'm not your parent, but I have read a great deal of medical research. The negative health effects of smoking cigarettes are so well documented that I personally believe it's suicidal to smoke. Millions of free radicals are released into the body by just one cigarette. If you currently smoke, I encourage you to find a way to quit. If you don't smoke...don't start! I definitely recommend that you avoid smoking in a business setting or at a business-related meal. Smoking can be highly offensive to those who don't smoke, and some people are physically allergic to smoke.

The subject of alcohol is just as tricky or trickier than the subject of smoking. Some people are able to drink alcohol safely and responsibly in moderate amounts. Even so, it is my experience that alcohol is an unwelcome and potentially destructive addition to any business discussion or relationship. As is the case with smoking, a person is rarely offended if you just say "no thanks" if you are offered alcohol. On the other hand, saying "yes" or drinking too much alcohol may cause offense. Drinking tends to loosen lips so that things are said and done that may later be regretted. Out of respect to people who have a physical problem with alcohol, as well as those whose family may have been impacted very negatively by alcohol, I recommend to make wise, responsible decisions in this area when in a business setting.

## 7. GET SUFFICIENT REST.

Contrary to what many people think, it is possible to achieve high levels of success and get sufficient sleep. There's never any real advantage in walking around half dead from a lack of rest.

The body needs rest. Some people may get by on only five to six hours a night, but that is the exception. Most people require at least seven hours of sleep a night, and some people as many as eight or nine hours of sleep.

Certainly there may be times when you need to burn a little midnight oil to get a project completed, but always recognize that the more sleep-deprived you become, the less productive and efficient you will be. The quality of your work may also suffer.

Oversleeping, or sleeping through an alarm clock, is nearly always a sign that you are under too much stress or you have poor nutrition. If your body is working correctly and your diet is right...if you have a healthy balance of work, play, and exercise...and if you are taking sufficient supplements and drinking enough pure, fresh water, you should awaken in the mornings with a high amount of energy, feeling fully alive and ready to take on the challenge of a day.

I often tell my business partners: Don't set a goal, and then fail to take care of yourself so that you never are able to enjoy the fruits of reaching that goal!

## Sufficient Preparation Is a Must!

Human beings obviously don't have the ability of a hummingbird to hibernate prior to undertaking a major challenge...but we do have the ability to plan in advance and to amass the resources we need to complete a project successfully. In order to fully prepare you must always:

# 1. KNOW WHERE YOU'RE GOING.

The hummingbird has a built-in sense of direction that carries it across miles of open water. You must have a clear picture of where you want to go and what you want to accomplish before you start a mission. You need to have an idea of what success looks like so you'll know when you have reached success! Having a strong sense of purpose and direction can give you energy and help sustain you over the long haul of the journey to the success you envision.

# 2. EVALUATE THE COST.

From a business standpoint, you need to calculate how much capital you'll need to complete a job. Ask:

- Do I have the necessary resources? If not, where might I get sufficient resources?

- Am I willing to make the sacrifices necessary—not only financially but in terms of sacrificing time doing other things?

- Have I taken into full consideration the "cost" of this venture in terms of the toll it might take on my family?

- Do I know the price of failure? (The hummingbird faces a very high cost of failure—falling dead into the ocean!)

When a young person decides to go to college and then on to graduate school to become a physician, lawyer, or scientist, that young person is usually very well aware of the time and money their "journey" toward an advanced degree is going to cost. When a person starts to build a house, that person is usually very well aware of the costs involved, as well as the time it will take to complete the house. New business ventures and expansions of current businesses present similar challenges. We should never start a project without first taking a look at both the timeline and projected budget for the successful establishment or completion of the project.

## 3. HAVE SUFFICIENT "FUEL."

The fuel required of a leader is more mental and psychological than physical. Keeping a vision alive in the face of criticism or discouragement can be very taxing on one's emotions. Ask yourself:

- Do I know how to fill my mind with the right input? Do I know where to get the information I need about my product and the business I'm pursuing?

- Am I willing to invest the time to listen to or to read educational materials that relate to what I am undertaking? Am I willing to "do my homework"? How do I get to people who have walked this journey successfully so I might learn from them?

- Can I find a coach or mentor who believes in me and can help me develop the life skills and business skills I need to become a leader? Am I willing to attend seminars or conferences, or to take short courses to develop specific skills?

If you are training to become a leader you must make a choice to associate with people who help fuel your energy and are a source of encouragement. Stay away from people who are

- Critical

- Overly protective to the point of discouraging you from taking all risks

- Jealous of your potential or present success

To help keep yourself on track, keep a journal in which you have written your goals and affirmations. Read to yourself every day the priorities and goals you have set for yourself. Reinforce your own dreams!

Practice visualizing the celebration of your success. Have a vivid picture in mind of what you might be doing once you have achieved your goal. This vision for your own future will energize and motivate you.

**ACTIVATING your will to fuel yourself and prepare yourself for the journey is what carries a person across the years... across the miles... and across the hurdles and obstacles... all the way to success.**

## The Longer the Journey

The longer the journey...the bigger the dream...the more noble the vision...the more you will need to stay well-fueled and prepared! You'll need energy to sustain your physical and emotional health. You'll need preparation to stay on track and stay "supplied" all the way to the goal. This is true in business, in the pursuit of an academic degree, in raising children, and for that matter, it is true in meeting any major challenge of life!

Having a will to win isn't what carries a person to success. ACTIVATING your will to fuel yourself and prepare yourself for the journey is what carries a person across the years...across the miles...and across the hurdles and obstacles...all the way to success.

**Belief alone is not enough.**

## THE GREAT BLONDIN

To walk on a tightrope across the great gorge at Niagara Falls even once seems foolish. To make this journey seventeen times might qualify as madness! That is exactly what the Great Blondin did.

The man known by this title was actually born Jean Francois Gravelet in 1824 in France. At the age of six he began his life in the circus and was known as "The Little Wonder." He traveled with the Ravel family of acrobats to America and soon became fascinated with the Niagara Falls gorge. He vowed to cross it on a high wire.

Eventually the Great Blondin found someone who would assist him in this challenge. A three-inch-diameter rope was stretched across the great gorge nearly one hundred and sixty feet—fifty meters—above the water. The distance across the gorge was a quarter of a mile—half a kilometer. Blondin not only crossed the gorge successfully, but then went on to attempt crossings with all kinds of stunts to make the crossing more daring.

On one crossing he wore a blindfold with a canvas sack over his head. On other crossings he ran, used stilts, and did acrobatic stunts, including standing on his head and doing summersaults. He once carried a stove to the halfway point on the rope, cooked an omelet for himself there, and ate the omelet before completing the crossing. At times he pushed a wheelbarrow in front of him while he crossed over, often boldly challenging onlookers to get in and go along for a ride.

In August 1859 Blondin carried his manager, Harry Colcord, across Niagara on his back. Broken guide ropes caused the main rope to swing violently and the terrified manager was forced to dismount halfway across.

Then in 1860 the Prince of Wales was present to watch a performance by the Great Blondin. He had heard of this man's daring feats and acrobatic skill. After successfully crossing the gorge to the predictable cheers of the crowd gathered, the Great Blondin turned to the Prince and asked, "So, do you now believe that I can do what they say?"

The Prince replied, "Yes, I believe."

Blondin then said, "If you really do believe, get in the wheelbarrow for the trip back across!"

The Prince, of course, remained silent and remained on dry ground.

The Great Blondin continued to perform his amazing feats well past the age of seventy! He toured Europe, duplicating for his audiences some of his famous Niagara high-wire acts. He died in his villa in 1897, after becoming quite wealthy as a result of his daring performances.

To my knowledge, no one ever got into his wheelbarrow.

# Would You Have Taken the Risk?

Countless people today observe the opportunities and accomplishments of other people and say, "I could do that" or, "That's definitely possible." Belief alone, however, is never enough to achieve a goal.

Too often people "believe" something is possible, but they never step out to take the risk and actually do what they profess to believe. It's more comfortable to stand on the sidelines than to get out on the playing field and put one's belief to the test. It's far easier to state a belief than to act on a belief.

**Belief alone is never enough to achieve a goal.**

Furthermore, it isn't enough to act on a belief just once. A genuine belief requires that we act on that belief repeatedly, often daily. Small acts of belief or faith—repeated frequently—are what create strength over time.

It didn't take much for people to stand on the banks of the Niagara Falls gorge and say they believed the Great Blondin would make a successful crossing. They had seen or heard about his previous successes. He obviously was talented, confident, and in a position to make good on his boasts.

What would have taken courage was for somebody to actually get in his wheelbarrow! It's at that point—when the challenge becomes personal with a definite upside and downside—that belief takes on a whole new dimension. It's at that point that belief is no longer an intellectual or emotional exercise—it is a risk.

The greater the challenge...the higher the stakes for failure...the greater the risk. And the greater the risk, the stronger one's faith must be.

It takes faith to take on any challenge or to take any risk, but the bigger the challenge, the greater the faith required!

This is true in business but also in other areas of life.

Consider the young couple that has been dating for a while and begins to discuss the possibility of getting married "someday." Both the young man and young woman might believe they love each other and that they are ready to marry. But then the question is asked and answered, the date is set, and the engagement ring is on the finger of the bride-to-be! Things change! Wedding plans begin to take shape. A cake and flowers are ordered, invitations are chosen and sent, the church is booked, the honeymoon is planned...and soon, what was once a generalized belief takes on the nature of a very personal and specific challenge! There's a risk involved. Greater and greater faith is required to follow through on that challenge.

A number of years ago we were traveling with friends on the south island of New Zealand. We came to a spot near Queenstown where the first bungee jumping took place. The bridge near Queenstown is about a hundred and forty feet above a magnificent gorge that has a fast-moving river. When we arrived at this location we found people who thought it was fun to jump off the bridge with their feet tied to an extremely elastic rope. They were willing to drop in a head-first free-fall manner to within just a foot or so of the river's surface and then bounce back up toward the bridge. The bouncing continued, of course, for several more falls until the person finally came to a "resting" position upside-down in the air just above the river. A small boat and its crew was waiting nearby to untie the elastic ropes and haul the person to safety.

At the time we were there the weather was cold and the wind was blowing. It was about 45 degrees Fahrenheit, but the water was colder than that! My friend Tony said to me, "Let's do it!"

I replied, "You must be crazy!"

He proceeded to tell me how safe it was and how much fun it would be.

He did his best to talk me into bungee jumping from the bridge but I wasn't at all willing to pay someone for the "privilege" of scaring myself witless. (I knew that if I was going to do something like that, I'd be sure to offer a very big tip to the person who adjusted and tied the ropes—a tip that would only be payable if I survived!)

In the end, my friend Tony made the jump! I was impressed. He not only survived but he enjoyed the thrill. I was impressed and excited for him. I became a "believer" that this was not only possible, but also a thrill. But did I jump? No. In the end, I didn't want the experience and the thrill badly enough to take the risk.

Can I say today that I believe bungee jumping can be a safe, fun activity? Yes.

Can I call myself a bungee jumper? No.

Believing in something is not the same as DOING something.

The pursuit of success always requires some risk-taking. It requires action. It requires the kind of believing that results in something actually being DONE.

If you truly have a goal...

If you truly have a desire that is worthwhile and compelling...

If you truly have a dream and vision for your life...

If you have a responsibility to your family or your team...

You MUST learn to operate as though failure is not an option. You must begin to run toward the goal that is set before you with all of your energy and focus.

## RISK AND RESPONSIBILITY

In no way am I encouraging you to be irresponsible in your risk-taking. Charging forward without a plan...without considering the costs...without evaluating the rewards... without having a clear vision of what you want to accomplish...is foolishness. What I am saying is that once you have responsibly considered an opportunity from all angles and determined that it is worth the risk, you MUST actually summon the courage to TAKE ACTION.

> **Once you have responsibly considered an opportunity from all angles and determined that it is worth the risk, you MUST actually summon the courage to TAKE ACTION.**

## A Performer or a Critic

One tongue-in-cheek definition of a critic is this: A person who evaluates a performance he can't give. There's little honor in simply pointing out the mistakes of others when you yourself have never attempted to do what the other person is doing.

There's also not much honor in being a bystander who "reports" what he sees others doing.

Through the years I have been fascinated, and at times irritated, and at other times mildly amused, by public speakers and authors of self-help books who share stories and ideas of success even though they have never faced the cold, hard realities of setting a personal goal and achieving it. A person who has only "studied" success and packaged a message about it—but who has never built a company or run a race or reached a concrete goal that requires leadership skills—may have some interesting theories, but virtually no credibility as far as I am concerned. I personally want to hear from people who have actually "been there, done that."

Charles "Tremendous" Jones once said that when he first got married he had three theories on how to raise children, but no children. Later, he said humorously, he had three children, but no theories!

It's easy to theorize, criticize, analyze, and even fantasize. It's something else to get in the wheelbarrow or to jump from the Queenstown bridge.

## And Just When You Decide to Make Your Move...

An interesting thing often happens just at the point where you summon your faith and your courage to make a positive move and act on your beliefs. A friend or co-worker—perhaps a close family member or a distant acquaintance—is likely to show up and warn you of dangers or predict your demise. It happens in nine cases out of ten! They may tell you that their intention is to "protect you"— even to protect you from yourself and your own ability to dream. They may tell you that they are offering advice because they love you—and in all candor, they love you but don't trust you. They may tell you that what you are doing will make you "different" or that you are putting yourself into a position to be ridiculed, rejected, or labeled a failure.

Your courage may make some people uncomfortable. They may be reminded in a subconscious way of their own fears and inability to muster courage. They may be jealous of the possibility you just might succeed in reaching your goal. They may have a hidden worry that if you are successful, you'll cease to love them or cease to spend as much time with them.

The decision you face when the "discouragers" and "doomsday predictors" show up is a very simple one: Are you going to become a leader or aren't you? Are you going to become an achiever or aren't you?

The truth is, if you want to live like others can't, you must do what others won't.

You must not only believe for a greater good and a higher purpose, you must act. And, you must act *regardless* of what others say to try to convince you to maintain the business-as-usual status quo of your life.

> **The truth is, if you want to live like others can't, you must do what others won't.**

## Once You Are in Motion

The good news is that once you have taken action and are "in motion" toward accomplishing your goals, things usually get much easier. You have far less time to agonize and theorize...you are now energized and actualized! There's work to do and that means no time to worry!

I like the story of the chicken and the pig who both saw the sign for a charity breakfast. The chicken said to the pig, "Hey, look! It's a great cause. They're serving bacon and eggs. Let's go in and make a contribution."

The pig thought for a moment and then said, "That's easy for you to say. Giving an egg is a contribution for you. Giving bacon for me means a total commitment!"

Successful completion of a goal always requires total commitment. But once you've made a commitment to pursue a goal, you'll find that a certain amount of momentum kicks in.

Two additional things happen as you work diligently with sold-out commitment. First, you find that you are no longer constantly aware of or preoccupied with the idea of "risk." You become far more aware of tasks that need to be done, people who need to be called, orders that need to be filled, processes that need to be put into place, and so forth. You become focused on the work at hand rather than the dangers that lurk in distant shadows.

Second, the more you work diligently with sold-out commitment, the less likely you are to be inclined to stop and listen to those who might criticize you or try to discourage you. You begin to realize that you know certain things that your critics and naysayers don't know and never will know: You know where you're going, what you'll do when you get there, and how much fun you'll have in both making the journey and reaping the rewards! You don't have time to listen to those who seek to discourage you. You have appointments to keep, tasks to do, and fun rewards to enjoy!

Today is the best possible day to get off the sidelines and onto your chosen playing field

No more watching and waiting.

Go for it!

**Learn to say, "Why not?"**

## PIANO ON THE
## BEACH

Not long ago I was on a business trip that took me around the world. From my home in Atlanta I flew westward across the United States and the Pacific Ocean to Korea, and then from there on to Europe, and from there southward across the African continent to the Republic of South Africa, and from there back to Atlanta. This is not an unusual trip for me to take, but this time, my son David went with me.

Korea was quite an adventure for David because he found himself with a computer in his room...but no bed! Welcome to the world of international ideosyncracies!

After Korea we flew to Thessaloniki, Greece, with brief stopovers in Singapore and Munich, Germany. When we landed in Germany—after some thirty-six hours of travel—I told David I wanted to go into the first-class lounge for coffee while we awaited the boarding call for our flight to Greece. I had been in the Lufthansa first-class lounge at the Munich airport a number of times before, but this time as I flashed my ticket and started into the lounge area, the woman at the entry desk said, "I'm sorry, sir, but you can't go in there. This is only for first-class passengers." I told her that I was aware of that, but that I was, indeed, booked in first class.

She took a look at my ticket and informed me that the upcoming leg of our trip—which was only the last hour or so of our very long journey from Korea—was booked as business class. I said, "Yes, I understand that. However, on this flight leg Lufthansa only offers business class. The rest of my around-the-world ticket is a first-class ticket on Lufthansa (that cost more than twenty thousand dollars). Surely one cup of coffee in the first-class lounge in Munich can be provided to a passenger who holds such a ticket."

Her answer was a very firm, "No. You must go down the hall and up the escalator to the business-class lounge."

I know the results of a poorly designed training system when I see one, and I had just been the victim of such a system! This woman knew the rules and felt responsible for enforcing them and there was NO way she was going to adjust even the slightest rule for the most reasonable of requests. The rules, from her perspective, were far more important than either common sense or good customer service. She was focused on the small picture of "doing a good job" and as a result, she had no concept of the bigger view of "serving a good customer."

There was no point in arguing further. I made a mental note and went out to buy coffee.

What happened to me in Munich happens every day in the business world. Very bad decisions are made by short-sighted, limited, and rigid people who put rules above service...focus on details and miss the big picture...and see only themselves to the exclusion of others.

I am sharing this incident with you only to give you a contrast to what David and I encountered the next day in Greece.

We were scheduled to host a seminar in the coastal city of Thessaloniki and we had built in a couple of days to adjust to the time-zone changes. We were told about a small boutique hotel right on the ocean. When we arrived, the attitude we encountered was dramatically different from what we had encountered in Munich—so much so that the difference was almost humorous.

The restaurant of this little hotel was closed during the afternoon hours, which is when we arrived to check in, but the manager of the hotel immediately asked, "What can I get you to eat?"

We asked, "What is available?"

He replied, "Whatever you want...we can get it."

"Really?" we said.

"Sure," he replied. "Why not?"

It only got better from there.

Did we want a massage? They offered massages on the rooftop overlooking the ocean.

Did we want a driver, a tour, or a special menu? It was all possible.

That night we went out to have an early dinner at a small-but-formal Italian patio restaurant overlooking the ocean. The meal was superb, the service was outstanding, and the view was beyond description. Our spirits were rejuvenated after the long trip. We were in a place of tremendous service, beauty, and possibilities! Every time we asked, "Is that right?" or, "Are you sure?" the response was, "Why not?"

When we got back to our hotel that night, I went out on the balcony of my room, which faced the beach. I noticed a glow of lights and peered over the edge of the balcony to see what was below. What I saw was a genuine surprise to me.

I travel a great deal and am rather routinely exposed to new, unique, and high-quality places and experiences. The scene below me, however, was something I had never seen before, and haven't seen since!

A table for two had been set up at the edge of the water. It had a white tablecloth, table candles, and a full setting of china and crystal. A waiter in a tuxedo with gloves was serving a couple who were sitting at the table on this Mediterranean beach. Four large iron candleholders were set up around their table, each with about twenty candles. And...there was a piano! Two of its legs were in the lapping water of the sea and two were on the sand. A man was playing beautiful romantic music. It was a sight one might only assume happens in the movies.

I saw the manager again the next morning and asked him about what I had seen. He told me that the couple at the table were guests from Spain who were celebrating their anniversary. They had asked for a romantic dinner on the beach and the manager was only too happy to arrange for that.

I asked him, "But how did you get the piano down that hill to the beach?"

He replied, "We carried it from the lobby." (That was a very long way.)

I said, "I can't believe you did that!"

He looked at me with a little smile and said, "Why NOT? My job is to make our guests happy."

What a contrast in attitude to that of the first-class lounge "keeper" in the Munich airport!

I have thought often of that manager and the hotel he runs.

What a business philosophy!

What a way to live!

Don't you love to see and experience excellence?

Don't you hate it when you are told that the rules "rule" and that reasonable requests aren't reason enough?

Don't you want to be around people and companies that look for ways to say, "Yes...why not?"

What kind of person are you? Can you visualize a piano on a beach and candles and a table setting for two? Can you see something special? Can you see how to go beyond the ordinary to provide the extraordinary?

## Become a "Possibility Person"

I love it when an attitude of "possibility" permeates a business or organization. The Nordstrom department stores are famous for their "heroic" customer service. This philosophy is built into their employee training and reward system. Nordstrom gives out awards internally to employees who have the best stories for serving a customer beyond the call of duty.

Let me give you an example of one of these stories. One day a woman went into one of the Nordstrom stores to return a set of automobile tires she felt was defective. The clerk at first tried to explain that Nordstrom does not sell tires. This, indeed, is true— Nordstrom sells clothing and clothing accessories. The woman insisted, however, that she bought the tires at Nordstrom and wanted them to honor their guarantee. After a minute or two, this alert salesperson realized that the best course she could take was to give the woman a refund. The woman exited the store very happy and only a few days later realized her mistake. She was very embarrassed and went back to make the situation right. The media heard about this store that actually went so far as to refund money for a product it didn't sell, and reported the incident widely.

Was this clerk's behavior crazy? Is the company policy crazy? Perhaps to the woman behind the Lufthansa desk in Munich—but not to someone who understands how to build a long-term business by looking for ways to say "yes" instead of "no." Customers like to hear the word "yes"!

Was this bad business? To the contrary! This story was no doubt worth millions of dollars to the company in terms of free publicity and public relations. Deservedly so!

As we have expanded our business worldwide and have opened offices in various nations, we have faced some interesting challenges in spreading our corporate philosophy and culture into some faraway places with strange-sounding names. Can you imagine the attitudes we faced fifteen years ago in places such as Indonesia, Hungary, Turkey, mainland China—we even faced major attitude differences in more cosmopolitan places such as Paris, London, and Tokyo.

At the time, many of our activities were taking place in nations that were just emerging from communism—and some had not yet emerged. People were accustomed to being told "no" and to being told exactly what to do and when. In many places the people had lived for many years with repressive governments, rampant corruption, and very little emphasis or teaching on values or capitalism.

We felt as if we were continually improvising. At times we felt as if one of our main tasks was to dodge the multitude of officials who were looking for a bribe before we could conduct a seminar in a public building. At times we had to search diligently for enough technicians, venues, or services that were in short supply. On more than one occasion we realized we needed to handle transportation for ten thousand to twenty thousand people and simultaneously speak to them in ten or more languages—imagine even trying to find that many headsets in Eastern Europe fifteen years ago!

One incident really stands out in my memory. I was scheduled to address a conference in the Czech Republic. The only hotel that was near our venue in the small city of Brno had no suites, and my staff felt that the work I had to do in that city required that I have a hotel suite. Between my speaking engagements, I was scheduled to meet with a number of people privately, and a small regular hotel room did not seem appropriate.

I didn't know any of this, however, until several months after the event. My very capable staff had quietly and persistently taken on the impossible.

When I arrived in Brno at the hotel I was escorted to my suite. I noticed that there was no number on the entry door, and that seemed a bit unusual. Then after I entered, I thought the configuration of the suite was a bit odd. There were four separate rooms and each had a bathroom. One was set up as a conference room, one as a sitting room, one as a bedroom, and one had a massage table.

What I learned later was that my staff had persuaded the hotel management to construct a suite by building a wall and doorway at the end of a hallway. The four rooms at the end of the hall became a "suite." Furniture was moved and rearranged. The end result was a bit odd, but entirely comfortable and useful. All of this had been completed just the night before I arrived!

My staff saw a problem...and found a solution! This is possibility thinking in action.

This same staff was responsible for a motto that has spread through our corporation worldwide. The motto came out of an exercise in creativity and problem-solving that my U.S. team was conducting during a management retreat. The goal of this particular exercise was to help people become solution-oriented and creative in a crisis.

The "crisis" this team dreamed up was this: Jim (me) had been speaking all day and long into the evening hours. Jim was very hungry. After the final event, late at night, he requested a pizza. (I realize that eating pizza late at night is not a very healthful thing, but this was the "old me" and the incident was hypothetical! Furthermore, this was supposed to be a humorous "pretend" incident for a hungry tyrant. In real life I would never have allowed such effort for such a trivial need!)

The question asked of the group at the management retreat was this: "What would you do to come up with this 'emergency pizza' for hungry Jim?" Some discussed checking all the restaurants in the area to see if they could order a pizza. Someone suggested asking one of the local people where a pizza might be purchased—perhaps someone knew of a storekeeper that wouldn't mind going in after hours to supply a pizza. Some suggested that I be offered a different food item. Some suggested hustling me back to my hotel room before room service closed for the night—or asking the hotel manager to keep the kitchen staff on duty. All of these seemed to be very expensive solutions, if not "unworkable."

Finally Milena, our manager from the Czech Republic, said quite excitedly, "I know! I would go home and make the pizza!" Everyone laughed and congratulated her on the simplicity and spirit of her solution. From then on, our teams regularly began to refer to MAKE THE PIZZA!

There is always a way to get results if you begin with a possibility attitude.

The manager at our hotel in Thessaloniki "made the pizza" when he put a piano on the beach.

Our team in Brno "made the pizza" when it created a hotel suite out of nothing in a day.

The people at Nordstrom "made the pizza" for a woman who returned tires for a refund.

Often our first reaction to challenges and problems is to see an impossibility. We never think to say, "Why not?" The big question to ask about that is obvious: "WHY NOT?" Solutions are always rooted in possibilities!

## Become an "Expectant Person"

Leaders set the tone for those who follow them. That's true for people in business as well as teachers, coaches, clergy, and parents. As a leader you must model a "Why not?" attitude of possibilities, or you will become a mere rule-repeater locked in impossibilities. If you truly are going to lead people into major growth and development, you need to help them take the lid off their thinking and become more creative, more solution-oriented, and more service-oriented.

The process of becoming a "possibility" person also leads to "expectant thinking."

People who approach problems as possibilities start to approach their own futures as being filled with "possibilities." They begin to dream bigger dreams and to expect more from themselves and from their efforts. They start "expecting" something big...something wonderful...something noble to happen.

You may never get what you "deserve" from life—but you usually do get what you expect. Expect to win!

# Begin to See and Expect Something Wonderful!

A few years ago we were considering a move to San Diego, California. We looked at a number of houses that didn't seem quite right, but then we stumbled on one house that our close friends thought would be perfect for us—and indeed, we loved it. The problem was that it was too expensive. The sellers wanted a million dollars more than what we wanted to pay.

**You may never get what you "deserve" from life—but you usually do get what you expect. Expect to win!**

I should tell you that the home had been professionally decorated and was beautiful, externally and internally. The view of San Diego's world-famous harbor and city skyline was unbelievably spectacular. We could see the world from the windows of that house—ships and sailboats in the harbor...Coronado Island... beaches...the city lights at night...and to the south, one could see all the way to Mexico on a clear day! If only the house had been less expensive.

We continued looking, but we never stopped talking about "that house." We could see ourselves living in it. We could close our eyes and see the view. After a year Nancy said, "Let's see if they have sold that house yet. If they haven't, maybe they've lowered the price by a million dollars!" I thought, *That wouldn't make any sense...prices have gone UP since then, not down.* Nancy persisted, however, until I made a call, and guess what? The owners were still looking for a buyer and just that week, they had lowered the price by...you guessed it, a million dollars!

What is it that you can "see" yourself doing? Where can you "see" yourself living? How big can you "see" your company growing?

Fifteen years ago, ninety percent of our business was in the United States but we began to visualize a "why not?" dream of having a thriving and expansive international business. We wanted to spread our dream to people around the world and to see what might be done in other cultures and nations. We had no infrastructure, no contacts, and no intelligent data with which to predict what might happen...but we could SEE IT! I could close my eyes and SEE stadiums full of people hungry to learn how to succeed in business. I could SEE people beginning to flourish and prosper in poverty-stricken nations. I could SEE people with a look of expectancy and hope on their faces. The vision was only in our minds and hearts...but that's where real "vision" happens. What you see is what you pursue...and ultimately, what you see IS what you get.

If you "see" nothing, you pursue nothing, and you get nothing.

If you "see" greatness, you pursue greatness, and you get greatness.

Today we enjoy seeing the world with our natural, physical eyes that we only saw in our "mind's eye" fifteen years ago.

Did we need to expand internationally? No. Over a span of twenty years, we had built a very solid and prosperous business in the United States. We were relatively comfortable in life. We weren't particularly eager to take on financial risk, the complexities of international accounting, and various tax and legal mazes. We had an "itch," however, to do something more. We could "see" it.

When we began to talk about our vision, a few pioneers from our U.S. base quickly joined us in taking on the challenge. We enjoyed great success with some remarkable entrepreneurs and visionaries in Australia who "ran with us." Our experiences and contacts with them led us to Europe, where we discovered more pioneers who were willing to take on the challenges, and from them, we gained contacts throughout the developing world—Eastern Europe, Turkey, and even into remote areas of Indonesia, India, Thailand, and Malaysia.

Have we finished expanding and growing? No! We can still "see" more!

The wonderful thing about "possibility" thinking and "expectant" thinking is that there's no end to possibilities, and therefore, no end to what one might expect!

## Moving Beyond Business

As we expanded our business around the world we became increasingly aware of social, educational, physical, and material needs that were beyond the world of business. We especially saw children in need. Working with a few of our key leaders, again in Australia, we began twelve years ago to consider ways in which we might use our influence and resources to help these needy children. We formed an alliance with World Vision, a well-known and highly respected public charity that supports children and worthy projects around the world.

Our first idea was to adopt a village in central Africa where the AIDS crisis was just beginning to be noticed. Remember, this was twelve years ago. At that time there were more than six thousand orphans in this one village in Uganda who had lost both parents to AIDS. We wondered what would happen if we could challenge each of our team members to sponsor just one child and direct the money to a specific village such as this one. It seemed overwhelming at first, but we could "see" such possibilities!

A special charitable fund was established called the "Network of Caring." Today, our team has raised more than twelve million dollars to help more than forty-five thousand children in Africa, as well as Turkey, the Philippines, India, Romania, and elsewhere. Network of Caring (NOC) has provided immunizations, health education, food, and agricultural supplies and tools. NOC has helped to build fifteen schools that serve more than twenty thousand students. It has made significant contributions to earthquake relief, refugee camps, and 9/11 relief funds, and has provided scholarships for higher education. The impact has been quite amazing to our family of entrepreneurs as well as to those in need.

Currently, Network of Caring, through its newly formed "Ambassador Fund," is building a first-rate school and housing for hundreds of street kids near Mumbai, India. The school will be self-supporting once it is completed. NOC for some years now has been the largest corporate supporter of children in World Vision's history.

Where did this all begin? In a moment of asking "Why not?" when we first had the idea of trying!

My son Eric has a possibility dream, too. A number of years ago, while we were living in San Diego, he was introduced to a sport called Power Soccer in which people play the game in powered wheelchairs. This opened up a world of possibilities for Eric!

Prior to Eric playing Power Soccer we had been unable to find any sport in which he might compete. Those who have certain disabilities such as cerebral palsy, muscular dystrophy, spina bifida, or spinal cord injuries often become very isolated from other people because of the great complications related to their transportation and care. Even in a large-population state such as California, only a few teams existed.

Later, when we moved to Atlanta and then Florida, Eric had no one with whom to play. So what did he do? He did what any possibility thinker would do—he decided to expand the sport to the entire United States. What a project that has turned out to be!

Starting Power Soccer teams is a challenge, in spite of the fact that the players love the sport. First, you need to find potential players—there are no master lists anywhere of those with injuries that require the regular use of a wheelchair. Then you need to find a coach who has knowledge of both soccer and power wheelchairs. You need enough players in a city to compete, enough money for some specialized equipment, a training program, and the list goes on.

Eric and a friend named Jerry, along with Eric's assistant and friend named David, went to work. They started teams in Atlanta, and then began traveling. They visited muscular dystrophy camps and followed up on leads to many cities across the United States. They raised money, often by spending hours each week in parking lots selling raffle tickets. They spoke to potential players to inspire the creation of teams.

Soon they had recruited another player, one of Eric's friends from California named Jesse, and he added another dimension of passion and commitment to the project. These young men spent months on the road and after three years of very hard work, their vision began to take shape. A national tournament was held in Indianapolis, Indiana, in June 2004. The event brought together one hundred and thirty-four wheelchair athletes from about twenty cities in the United States. People who are confined to power chairs often do not get to meet more than one or two other people in their entire lifetime who are in their same situation. At that one event, people were able to see and make friends with dozens of others who shared their circumstances—but who also were people of possibility!

In addition to the teams from the United States, "all-star" teams from France and Japan came to Indianapolis.

Seeing all of these young people playing their hearts out and receiving trophies at the closing ceremony, which was followed by a big dance party, is something I will never forget...nor will they! The event will be held annually and the number of teams continues to grow. Eric and his friends are thinking big—they hope to be able to demonstrate the sport at the Beijing Olympics in China in 2008 as part of the Para-Olympic competition. Their goal is to see Power Soccer become an "official sport" at the 2012 Para-Olympic Games. The Ambassador Fund is committed to helping them achieve their dream.

Lives have been "improved," new experience has been provided, and memories and relationships have been created for hundreds of young people through this program. And where did it begin? It began with "why not?" thinking.

As the Power Soccer program began to develop, Nancy and I started a charitable organization known as "The Fernando Foundation." This foundation is in memory of Eric's first assistant, Fernando Ruelas, who died suddenly of leukemia at age thirty. Fernando was passionate about helping people with disabilities. He believed in our son Eric and in the "possibilities" of his life. His brother David is now with our family and serves as the executive director of The Fernando Foundation. David leads the effort to raise money to assist the disabled in physical and spiritual ways. More than two hundred thousand dollars has been raised for this foundation. Many of those who are helped are people "discovered" through the Power Soccer network. David and the others involved in The Fernando Foundation have a goal of raising one million dollars over the next few years. "Why not?" they ask![5]

# And What About You?

In what area of your life do you need to begin to ask, "Why not?"

Perhaps the challenge before you is a marriage, a new career, or starting a business of your own. It might be the challenge of setting a higher career goal or beginning a charitable project.

What possibilities do you SEE?

What can you begin to EXPECT?

Are you capable of seeing a dinner on a beach, complete with a piano?

Do you see a cause you can influence or assist?

Do you have an exciting idea that you can't seem to get out of your mind?

Do you wonder what might be possible, in spite of the "facts"?

Put your vision into sharp focus. Begin to see it as a reality. Think in terms of "details" and "full color" and "exciting motion"! Ask yourself some expansive questions:

- What would you do if you had a million dollars or the ability to raise that amount?

- What if you had a year off to do whatever you desire with whomever you want?

- Who would you help if you could help someone?

- What if you could have it "all"—what would "all" look like?

- What would you change if you could change something?

A person who has time but no money can't do much. A person who has money and no time is both frustrated and limited. Having time and money, with nothing worthwhile to fill the time or do with the money, is a huge waste.

Actor Jim Carrey relates that long before he was making serious money in films, he wrote out a fake check to himself for twenty million dollars. He looked at that check regularly. He visualized working in films and making that much for each one. You probably can guess the rest of the story. He is now regularly paid twenty million dollars for every film in which he stars.

Why not write an imaginary check to yourself...or to a cause you believe in...for an amount that both challenges and motivates you? Look at that check daily. Ask yourself, "Why not?"...and then go for it!

Start thinking "out of the box" about each worthy request, unrealized dream, or new challenge that presents itself to you. Begin to SEE what might be done.

Your fresh thinking and creative ideas will not only bring you joy, but you will be an inspiration to others.

If you think something is possible...you are right.

If you think something is impossible...you are also right.

> **If you think something is possible...you are right.**
> **If you think something is impossible...you are also right.**

Ask yourself today, "Why am I settling for a cold sandwich in a dumpy café when I might be enjoying a candlelight dinner on a beach in Greece with piano music filling the air?"

Why ARE you settling for something far less than the finest possibility you can envision?

1  Luke 12:48

2  Matthew 7:24–25

3  Matthew 22:37–39

4  Matthew 6:19–21

5  To contribute to Network of Caring, contact:

   World Vision Network of Caring

   P.O. Box 9716

   Federal Way, Washington 98063-9716

   USA

   www.worldvision.org

To contribute to The Fernando Foundation or the Ambassador Fund, send contributions to:

Fernando Foundation

3550 Corporate Way-Suite C

Duluth, Georgia 30096

USA

1 (800) 847-4274

www.fernandofoundation.org

e-mail: afinfo@ambassadorfund.org